TWIXT TYNE AND TWEED

*The story of a walk from Tynemouth to Berwick
told in prose, poetry and paintings.*

Kathleen and Harry Gilbert

Also by
Kathleen Gilbert

'Shades of Lakeland'

A description of favourite walks in Borrowdale
together with paintings, sketches and original poetry.

'A delightful tribute to a much loved valley'
'An album of memories and moments decorously captured in word and image'
'Evocative, at times lyrical'

Keswick Reminder

9 780954 349110

Copyright Kathleen Gilbert 2003

Published by 'Glaramara Studios'
Printed by 'Penny Print' Blaydon
First Edition 2003
ISBN 0-9543491-1-3

FOREWORD
Twixt Tyne and Tweed
By Rt. Hon. Alan Beith, M.P.

I feel as if I have made a lifetime's journey along the route of the walk which is so vividly described and beautifully illustrated in these pages. In the 1960's I lived in Hotspur Street, Tynemouth, just beside the start of this walk: for the last decade and a half I have lived in Castle Terrace, Berwick, near where the walk ends. The very street names speak of the county's wonderful history and its castle-studded coastline. It is a shoreline of staggering beauty, and at the same time the home of past and present industries: shipping and shipbuilding; coal-mining and aluminium smelting; power stations and wind farms; fishing, farming and food processing, tourism and leisure.

In this cradle of English Christianity monks decorated the Lindisfarne Gospels, John Knox preached a Presbyterian gospel in Berwick, John Wesley addressed the folk of Alnwick and Holy Island, and brown-habited Fransciscan friars still walk the sands of Alnmouth, and in politically calmer times we can recall that in 1826 two election candidates, a Lambton and a Beaumont, fought a duel on Bamburgh beach.

Golf courses, including some of oldest in England, are numerous, bird watchers flock to the Farnes, and bright yellow helicopters from RAF Boulmer search for the lost on sea and land, and remind us that there is still a significant military presence, with the station's radar and fighter control activities fulfilling the defensive role that the castles once played. For much of the county's length, the main East Coast railway line runs close to the shore and gives travellers breathtaking glimpses of Alnmouth, of Cocklawburn beach and of the Tweed meeting the sea. The industry and activity by which the area has earned its living has only rarely damaged and has never taken away the stunning beauty of the Northumberland Coast, so much of which is totally unspoiled, and Northumberland it is which this walk describes — the historic county embraced every step of the way from Tynemouth to the north banks of the Tweed, save only for what was once a far flung outcrop of Durham beside Holy Island, still known as Islandshire. An amazing walk: an amazing county.

Alan Beith

Dedication

**This book is dedicated to those brave people, past and present,
who have risked their lives to save others off the North Sea Coast**

Acknowledgements

We would like to thank those people who have assisted us in various ways, supplied us with valuable information,
taken the time to talk to us and generally given us encouragement in this project.

We would like to acknowledge the following sources of reference

'Northumberland' A book produced by Northumberland Education Committee
to mark the Coronation of Queen Elizabeth II

The 'Northumbrian' magazine

'Those Delavals' by Roger Burgess published by Frank Graham

'Cullercoats Artists' An exhibition at the Laing Art Gallery Newcastle-upon-Tyne

'Grey of Fallodon' by G.M. Trevelyan O.M. published by Longmans, Green & Co.

'A History of the English Speaking People' by Sir Winston Churchill published by Castell & Co Ltd. London

'The Scottish Border and Northumberland' by John Talbot White published by Eyre Methuen. London

Waiting in our bright green Tensons
for the tide to clear the Holy Island causeway

Kathleen Gilbert, a retired headteacher, was born in Leeds but has long been a 'naturalised' Northumbrian.

Harry, her husband, has lived all his life in Northumberland and worked as a Local Government Officer in the area until his retirement.

As a couple they are widely travelled but have always retained their love for this wonderful county and, in particular, its magnificent coastline.

CONTENTS

		PAGE			PAGE
Pre-Amble		1	Day Four	Craster to Bamburgh	55
Day One	Tynemouth to Newbiggin-by-the-Sea	9	Day Five	Bamburgh to Holy Island	67
Day Two	Newbiggin-by-the-Sea to Warkworth	29	Day Six	Holy Island to Berwick	83
Day Three	Warkworth to Craster	41	Foot-note		90

PAINTINGS

	PAGE		PAGE
The Mouth of the Tyne	7	The Bathing House	51
St. Mary's Island	17	Craster Harbour	53
The Harbour - Seaton Sluice	21	Dunstanburgh Castle	57
St. Bartholomew's Church, Newbiggin	31	Bamburgh Castle	69
Alnmouth	43	Lindisfarne	77
Boulmer	47	Berwick-on-Tweed	87

CONTENTS CONTINUED

POEMS

	PAGE		PAGE
Leaving the Tyne	6	The Bathing House	50
St. Mary's Light	16	A Safe Return	52
Seaton Sluice	20	Dunstanburgh	56
St. Bartholomew's Church	30	Bamburgh Castle	68
Alnmouth	42	Lindisfarne	76
Lost At Sea	46	On Seeing Berwick-on-Tweed	86

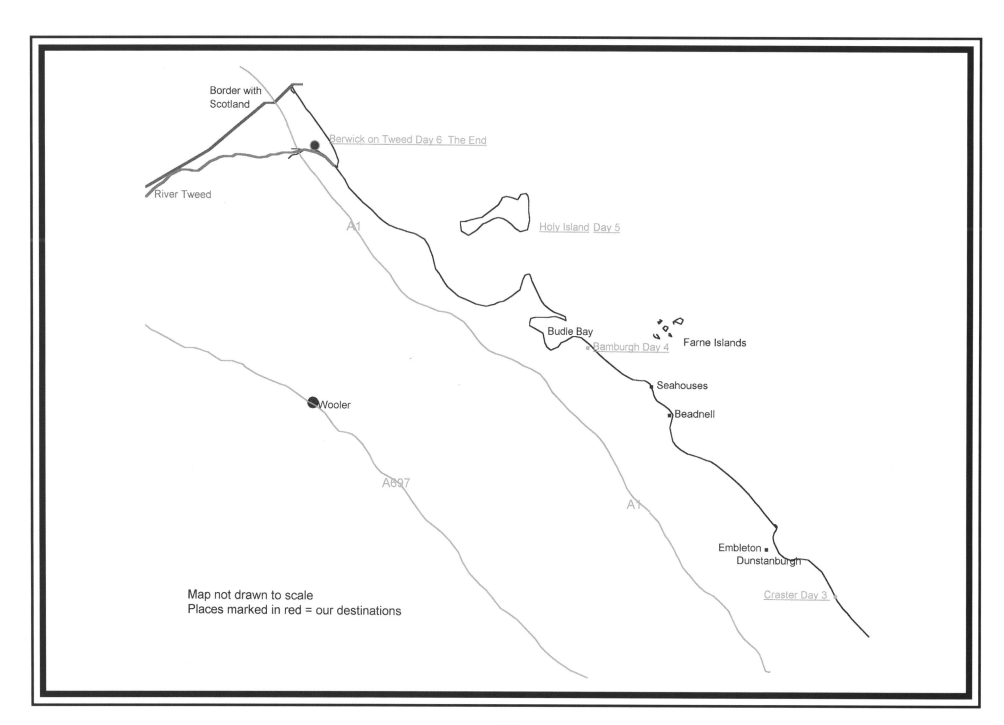

Border with
Scotland

Berwick on Tweed Day 6 The End

River Tweed

A1

Holy Island Day 5

Budle Bay

Farne Islands

Bamburgh Day 4

Seahouses

Wooler

Beadnell

A697

A1

Embleton
Dunstanburgh

Map not drawn to scale
Places marked in red = our destinations

Craster Day 3

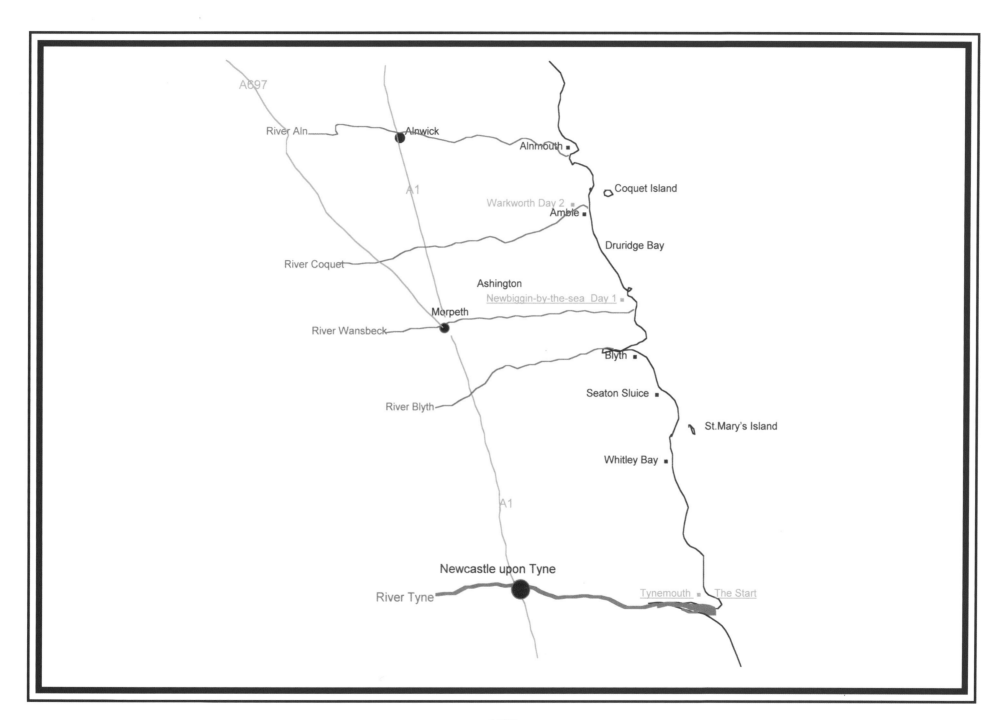

TWIXT TYNE AND TWEED

PRE-AMBLE

I love reading travel books particularly those about real adventures and I journey with my characters to wild and exotic parts of the world. On one of these armchair travels, I read 'Clear Waters Rising' by Nicholas Crane and wondered at his commitment to travel on foot from Finisterre to Istanbul via all the high mountain ranges. I admired his purist ideals of not accepting mechanical means of transport even to the point of not using a chair lift in the Alps when the excursion was not even on his route. I liked the idea of moving on, creating a continuous picture and being responsible to no-one except oneself. It seemed like a brave challenge to me and one which I would like to echo. There are now many long distance footpaths in Britain, mapped and well documented. I could use one of these as my blue print but they are walked by thousands every year. I was looking for something a little more personal.

The Northumberland Coast is a largely unknown jewel in the coastal coronet of Britain but there are many sections well loved of Northumbrians and much visited.

How did these jigsaw pieces fit together? What happened to the coastline in between?

We had walked much of the Coast in short snatches but it would be good to connect those sections in a continuous whole. I accepted that I was no Nicholas Crane, that this was not a high altitude escapade and the purist ideals of not accepting mechanical means of transport were soon sacrificed to the God of practicalities, but Nicholas had kindled in me the desire to try something different. I needed company on my walk so I set to work to persuade my husband Harry that this would be an interesting project. After a bit of coaxing he agreed and we started to plan our journey.

What would our objective be? To the north and south, Northumberland has two clear boundary marks in two rivers flowing into the North Sea, the Tyne in the south and the Tweed in the north. The old seafaring town of Tynemouth stands at the mouth of the Tyne and Berwick, on the river Tweed, marks the natural boundary with Scotland.

These seemed to be obvious starting and finishing points; the distance Twixt Tyne and Tweed approximately 70 miles. Not a marathon, but for we novices it would be enough.

Preparations began. How far would we walk in a day? Should we book accommodation? How much could we carry ? As we worked on distances we realised that some areas of our walk would have a glut of possible places to stay while others offered little in the way of accommodation. I decided that it would be interesting to stay on Holy Island and be there when the tide closed the causeway. What would the island be like when the tourists had gone home ? It would only take one large event such as a wedding and all rooms on Holy Island could be taken so we decided it would be necessary to book our room there. Having one fixed night meant that the rest started to fall into place and it seemed sensible to book all our accommodation. We wanted to travel as light as possible so decided on layers with thermals and cotton trousers, shorts and waterproofs which would also act as a windproof layer. The week before we set off was very wet. As one rainy day followed another we wondered about footwear. Soft boots would soon be saturated if it continued to rain. Leather boots could become damaged in sea water - we settled for trainers, a big mistake for me.

There were some potentially difficult or boring sections of the route to negotiate. The River Blyth does not have any bridges in the town, so to cross it would mean a lengthy walk through Blyth to the A189 and then back to the coast at Cambois, something like seven miles in all. There used to be a ferry across the river to North Blyth but this has ceased to operate, so it looked as though we were destined for a long detour. Other estuaries, the Wansbeck, the Lyne, and the Aln, would create similar, though less demanding problems.

Our good friend Ian Gray is ever the pessimist and when we described our plan to him he declared that we must be mad. It would rain every day….we'd never make it and what did we want to do that for when we could go to places quite easily in the car. Despite his protestations he agreed to drive us to the start of our walk.

Two days before we set off we went down to Tynemouth to 'psych' ourselves up for our adventure. I'd just started reading 'The Watch House,' a book for young adults by Robert Westall, based on the coast guard station at Tynemouth. I'd visited the station many years ago and was curious to see if it was as I remembered it, a glorious collection of memorabilia. 'Lets go and have a look,' I said to Harry.

Bill Scott was polishing the knocker on the big front door when we met him. A small man with burnished cheeks and a bristly beard.

'Is there an entry fee?' I enquired.

'No lass, just a donation to our rescue service. We're the oldest station in the country.'

We went into a room full of memorabilia and gleaming brass, smelling of beeswax polish.

'Aye we've a lot of stuff but it all means something-it's all genuine (pronounced American fashion). HMS Brave rescue - we still use the teapot' and he went away and returned with a large aluminium teapot. He rubbed near the lid and pointed out an inscription - HMS Brave - 1951

'Aye and it's older than that-it would be around during the war. We've applied for a grant ye knaa. Thought we would get it straight away being a rescue service - 863 lives saved - but they're a funny lot like - it's all bureaucracy - all forms to fill in. These drums now.. they've all saved a life…Aye, there was a schooner got into difficulties. Man had his five year old daughter on board. He got a plank and lashed it to this drum and she was dragged by the tide into The Haven. All drowned except her. She became an honorary member.'

On the wall were ships' nameplates, all from ships whose crews had been rescued.

'Seven Sons', 'Amalie', 'Drogheda'.

'Are you sea-going then?' he asked.

'No…no I'm seasick going to the Farnes,' Harry replied ruefully.

'Sea sickness, aye it's deadly nightshade. I emigrated to Australia - lived there 21 years.'

'Why did you come back?'

'Women trouble…'

'What? A girl in every port?' I teased.

'Aye and more than that….' He chuckled. 'Their men didn't like it. Hard lot them Aussies. So I came home.'

We gazed at two figure heads arranged, along with some other decorative work, on the end wall of the room.

'Beautiful ladies that they nivver got, poor buggers. And that's the figurehead from 'The Star of the Sea' and 'The Horn of Plenty'. I used to like to fire the maroon….boom. Oh it was exciting but its gone now - kaput.'

There was a breeches buoy strung across the room. I gave it a closer inspection. I'd never appreciated why they were called breeches buoys. A piece of canvas rather like some oversized cropped breeches was fastened to ropes and pulleys.

'Antiquated maybe, but effective. According to Europe they're not safe - we shouldn't be using them. Never mind how many lives they've saved'

'So what do you use instead?' I asked.

'Helicopter. But there's places they can't get to with a helicopter. A lifeboat can get in with just two feet of water. All they think about now - bloody money.'

We left thinking of sea rescues and the brave traditions of those who plucked souls from the peril of the seas. I hadn't appreciated how many shipwrecks had occurred off the Northumberland Coast and how dangerous our coastline has been. Grace Darling may be the person remembered for her brave rescue but she is almost a figurehead symbolising many men and women who risked their lives for others.

Outside, we walked along the cliff path and saw a new addition - a sign pointing north.....Berwick 72 miles it said.

There it was - our challenge. On Thursday we would be setting off.

The Watch House

Tynemouth was the first volunteer life brigade in the country. It was formed by John Morrison and Joseph and John Spence in 1864 after thirty four lives were lost when three ships, 'The Ardwell', 'Stanley', and 'Friendship' came to grief during easterly gales. Since then, members have saved the lives of many sailors whose ships have been wrecked on the Black Middens, or the Spanish Battery rocks near the mouth of the Tyne.

Memorabilia from wrecks is displayed in the Watch House. Standing behind the motley collection of houses is a statue of Admiral Lord Collingwood. The hill below is a good vantage point, an ideal position to view events such as The Tall Ships Race.

Leaving the Tyne

Priory ruins by purple shadows cowled,
Stand proudly on their promontory,
Morning scatters silver coins of sunlight
On the ruffled velvet of the Tyne.
Ships slip seaward through these piers
To meet the daunting vastness of the ocean,
Departing with, 'God Speed,'
We wish you safe return.
Gone, gone to far horizons.

Black Backed Gulls

8

**Day 1
Tynemouth to
Newbiggin-by-the-Sea**

The day dawned dull and overcast. It looked as though Ian was going to be right. It was rush hour for everybody else and as a retired teacher, I felt slightly naughty to see children and teachers going to school, rather like playing hookey.

We got out of the car at the top of the cliffs and looked out to sea between the two arms of the protective piers of North and South Shields. The sea was calm and misty. Behind us stood the lofty memorial to Admiral Lord Collingwood who seemed to peer down at us from the top of his column. He led the British fleet into action at the battle of Trafalgar. 'Whenever I think how I am to be happy again, my thoughts carry me back to Morpeth. How I long to have a peep into my home and walk in my own garden. It is the pleasing object of all my hopes.' But he never saw home or family again despite the fact that he lived for five years after Trafalgar. An English sailor and a just and kindly man. An adventurer who never returned but we expected that in a week we would be re-united with our beloved home and family.

Ian took our photograph at the top of the cliffs. Harry entitled this one, 'Putting a brave face on it,' and then we said goodbye, waving as we watched Ian's car leave the Haven car park. We were alone at the start of our adventure. Next stop Newbiggin-by-the-Sea. I suddenly became aware of all the aches and pains I'd ever had; my back was giving twinges, that tooth was nagging, had I the beginnings of a headache? All reasons to give in…to chicken out. But we put it all behind us and made ready to set off.

We looked out over the mouth of the Tyne marked by the two piers of North and South Shields. North Shields pier is longer and bears the brunt of crashing waves from the north which break right over the walls. On such days it is closed to fishermen and promenaders. It's exciting to stand on the rocky headland between the two and look out to sea, maybe watching a North Sea Ferry set off for Norway or a small yacht from the sailing club brave rough seas as it crosses the bar to find shelter in Tynemouth Haven, a small sandy bay at the foot of the headland. Towering above North Shields pier, on a sandstone cliff, are the remains of a castle and priory. Great lancet windows are silhouetted against the sky. There have been monastic buildings here for 1,300 years, many of them destroyed by Viking raiders.

In 1100 the Priory was rebuilt and became the cell of Benedictine monks from St. Albans. They were known as black monks because they wore dark coloured robes. They didn't like the north east and many were sent to Tynemouth as a punishment. One monk wrote to his friend at St. Albans saying, 'Our house is confined by the sea on every side but one…Day and night the waves break and roar and undermine the cliff.

Thick sea frets roll in wrapping everything in gloom. Dim eyes, hoarse voices, sore throats are the consequence. Spring and summer never come here. The north wind is always blowing and brings with it cold and snow; or storms in which the wind tosses the salt in masses over our buildings and rains it down within the castle. Shipwrecks are frequent. See to it, dear brother, that you do not come to so comfortless a place.'

This impregnable site was used for defence purposes during Mediaeval times when a castle was built and then during the first and second world wars when gun emplacements were created on the headland. An impregnable position with rough seas crashing at its feet, it made an ideal venue for an open air performance of 'The Tempest' which we saw two years ago.

King Edward's Bay

The shipwreck was enacted on the coastal battery at the farthest point on the headland. Actors shouted to make themselves heard above the cries of fulmars and kittiwakes and the roar of the waves. Very atmospheric.

In the shadow of Tynemouth Priory and Castle lies a charming sandy bay scooped out beneath the cliffs - King Edward's Bay. Robert Jobling, one of the Cullercoats' colony of artists, painted this scene in moonlight. Above the promenade is a pub, The Gibraltar Rock, which has a restaurant overlooking the bay, a delightful location.

We walked up the steep bank from The Haven and past the castle which stands at the head of Tynemouth Front Street, where we read a plaque which told us that this headland used to be known to the Saxons as Pen Bal Craig - Head Summit Rock - and that three kings were buried here; Oswin of Deria, Osred of Northumbria and Malcolm III of Scotland. Tynemouth's coat of arms bears three crowns in memory of these kings.

Tynemouth is positioned between the industry of the Tyne and a now faded seaside resort but its Front Street contains a selection of reasonable shops, cafes and pubs and there is a selection of accommodation in the area. A number of famous people have lived here including Harriet Martineau, the novelist, who was visited by among others, Thomas Carlyle and Charlotte Bronte.

Beyond Front Street is Percy Gardens, a beautiful collection of Edwardian houses now turned into apartments, all with expansive sea views. Gulls wheeled and squawked. We said 'Good Morning' to dog walkers and men out for their morning constitutional, were passed at speed by keep-fit freaks having their obligatory jog and the not so speedy old dears being pushed out in their wheel-chairs from the local care home. As we rounded the headland a wide sweep of golden sand, bordered by gently breaking waves, came into view - Tynemouth Long Sands. At the far end was the spire of St. George's Church, dark and prominent. Full of determination we marched towards it. Here, below the faded opulence of the Grand Hotel, was the site of an open air bathing pool. My family and I once went to a bathing beauty contest here - bathing beauties, now they're a thing of the past. Imagine parading along the catwalk in a bathing costume in our North Eastern summers. How ridiculous!

Plastic swans bobbed lonely and cold on the children's boating pool in Tynemouth Park. Then, as we passed the Park Hotel on the front, I jokingly said, 'We could call at Henley Road for a cup of coffee.' Henley Road is where Ian and Gloria live.

Rounding the point we came to Cullercoats Bay, an almost perfect saucer sheltered by two piers. All along the front were elegant turn of the century houses now converted to B&B's, with salty, seaworthy names like, 'Creel House', 'Beacon House', 'Monks' Haven'. Former Life Brigade premises have been converted into a garage but with the name of 'Rocket Garage' we were left wondering what sort of vehicle they serviced - very futuristic.

The Rocket Garage

The building was used to store Life Brigade equipment including rockets and lines. Down below the promenade lies the Dove Marine Laboratory, founded in 1897 and owned by Newcastle University. It is a major centre for teaching and research into the marine environment. Large aquaria and deep tanks of sea water make fish and sea creatures available for study.

Amusement arcades have robbed Cullercoats of its atmosphere of a small fishing community. I remember rows of white cottages where fishwives sold shellfish and crabs from their doorstep. Windows were frilled with net curtains, and clippy mats were just visible in the dark interiors. Fishwives like Polly Donkin, Bella Jefferson, and Lizzie Taylor could be seen wearing their traditional shawls and ankle length skirts. Sadly the cottages were demolished in the 1960's to be replaced by modern apologies. Had they survived into another decade they may have been retained as part of Cullercoats' natural heritage and become museums.

During the 19th century a colony of artists based themselves in Cullercoats. Their aim was to paint Cullercoats' people, recording their life and times as truthfully as possible. They painted canvases showing landing and selling the catch, sea rescues depicting the heroism of lifeboat men, scenes on the beach during their holiday times and moments of sadness when lives were lost.

'Men must Work and Women must Weep', was the title of one very moving painting. The Daily Leader of 1887 said, 'Cullercoats has now established its reputation as the great painting ground of the North East Coast,' but the Newcastle Journal thought that the artists would make Cullercoats famous, and by-and-by the village would be over-run with tourists. Ralph Hedley, Isa and Robert Jobling and John Falconer Slater, who has been likened to Whistler and Manet, were members of the group. Slater enjoyed painting rough seas and could often be seen, with his large eight by five feet canvas, down on the rocks. He had to hire a man with a flat cart to transport his canvas and easel down to the promenade and use guy-ropes to secure his equipment. Slater was colloquially called 'the weatherproof artist.' He once recorded, 'The wind increasing in violence nearly blew the canvas, easel and moorings away. I do not remember having had a harder or more thrilling tussle.'

Rounding the point from Cullercoats we could see our first landmark of the day - St. Mary's Island. It was nearly coffee time and we tried to cadge a cup from workmen in their cabin but the breeze caught their reply and flung it away from us so we continued down the naturally made steps to the promenade.

Fulmars were nesting in the cups, shelves and hollows along the cliffs. The smell of seaweed pervaded the air. We pressed on past the Rex Hotel with glass fronted additions to its former posh exterior. Its glories having faded and crumbled, it is now starting a new lease of life. We looked for toilets on the Whitley Bay promenade but the Council must believe that it is only men who are 'caught short' because the 'ladies' was firmly locked. Harry kept lookout for me while I went to use the 'gents'. Think this was a first!

We made our way onto the red and cream checked promenade. I remember the beach here being crowded with hoards of children, many of them gathered round 'Sunshine Corner', a type of religious mission for youngsters. Their voices seemed to echo from the past. 'Jesus wants me for a sunbeam…' Whitley Bay Bathing Club always go for a New Year's Day swim from the beach near here - rather them than me. The Venetian Café, where I had hoped we might have a coffee or perhaps an ice cream, came into view. I was disappointed to discover that it was closed. There seemed to be somebody inside. He made a sign holding up five fingers on one hand. I suppose he meant, 'Open in five minutes'. He pointed to the side window and opened it. When he spoke it was with an Italian accent - our first genuine Geordie Italian - just like his ice cream Italian style 99. We licked happily and walked on. Links Avenue, my home during my teenage years, was just across the grass. In those days I could see the flash of St. Mary's Lighthouse on my bedroom wall.

I spent many happy hours here on the beach, sometimes sitting against the sea wall revising for exams. A man called Mr. Lawson used to stable beach ponies in a field at the top of our street. On Sunday mornings during the winter he would allow local children to ride his ponies along the beach. In the melee when he opened the corral gate and we surged forward trying to claim our favourite mount, I always tried to get a particular pony which was supposed to have Arabian ancestry - it was the smartest and liveliest of the bunch. Despite not having riding skills, I seemed to cope, even when we attempted a canter or gallop. We walked on to where the promenade came to an end when we took the cliff path up to the Briar Dene car park. Here we looked back at Whitley Bay with its strange Moorish white dome, The Rotunda or Spanish City. In its hey-day, Whitley Bay was a thriving resort, especially during Scots' week when hoards of holiday makers from across the border descended on the town to make merry. All the hotels and boarding houses were full, there was country dancing in Panama Dip, tea dances in the Rotunda Ballroom and the rides in the Spanish City fun-fair spun screaming youths on into the night. Now the fun-fair has been demolished and the amusement arcades boarded up.

Whitley Bay must find a new role for itself.

Whitley Bay from the cliff top

Our path led between the miniature golf course and the edge of clay cliffs which are gradually being eroded by sea and rain. A road runs along the headland to popular St. Mary's Island, linked to the mainland by a short causeway which is covered by sea for four hours twice a day. The tide was out and people were going across to visit the lighthouse or to peer into the deep rock pools for signs of marine life. St. Mary's Island, or Bait Island, is off what used to be known as Curry's Point where Michael Curry was executed and hung from a gibbet for the murder of the landlord of the Three Horseshoes Inn at Hartley. There was no hint of such dark and dismal deeds today as the sun had come out and the larks were singing in the sunshine. A flock of sanderling got up and flew in a skein of light against a dark cloud. They twisted and turned, visible and invisible, lost and found. Suddenly they scattered and re-appeared as a multitude of stars, like the flowering of a rocket on bonfire night . A moment I'll treasure in my memory.

The lighthouse was built in 1898 to prevent ships running aground on the rocky island. Two cottages were provided for the keepers of the light but in 1984 St. Mary's was decommissioned by Trinity House and its future became the subject of local debate. People of Whitley Bay consider the lighthouse to be an icon, part of the town's character, so, as a public institution, they did not want to see it pulled down or pass into private ownership. Thankfully it has been made into a visitor centre with facilities for school groups to study marine life. 27,000 people a year climb 137 steps to gain a view from 'the light' . A café and souvenir shop occupy the houses which once belonged to the lighthouse keeper.

I can remember as a child, peering into the deep channels and pools looking for sea life. There were crabs, sea urchins, star fish, sea anemones and a variety of different types of seaweed. A fascinating place. This is now part of a designated Marine Nature Reserve covering the rocks, cliffs and foreshore.

We looked in at St. Mary's Nature Reserve, a protected piece of fresh water which attracts autumn and spring migrants. There was a coot on her nest, oystercatchers performing a bobbing dance, a tufted duck with shining amber eye drifting past and lapwings wheeling above the windswept waters. Beyond St. Mary's Island the cliff path dips and winds above rocky outcrops. Wild flowers blossom amongst the grass. Today there were royal purple bee orchids and delicate white milkmaids. Views of the lighthouse were fringed with 'old man's baccy.'

Hereabouts is a small car park with a track leading up to the main road. If you are in need of sustenance there is a pub, The Delaval Arms, at the junction. We continued on the cliff top path leading out of the car park and along to Collywell Bay, once famous for its red sandstone stack nick-named Charlie's Garden.

St. Mary's Light

Two flashes on my bedroom wall
Then the giant lantern turns
Spilling darkness
Into eyes
Leaving
Dark shadows lurking
Threatening my childhood world.
Seventeen, eighteen, nineteen, twenty.
Light revolves, reveals
My bed, my chair,
My teddy bear.

Another searchlight beam
Begins its progress through my room,
Panning with relentless eye
My books, my gown,
My eiderdown.

Then gone
And I'm alone.

Kathleen Gilbert

Sadly the stack has been gradually eroded by the sea and little now remains. Six kilns, used in glassmaking, used to stand at the end of the bay and were a landmark for miles around. They were built by Sir John and Thomas Delaval and used copperas, a by-product of coal mining, to colour the glass bottles which were made there. The Delavals also owned seventeen mines in the area including the Hartley Pit which produced a coal which burned particularly well. I took a photograph of the remains of Charlie's Garden and a man collecting coal on the beach. This used to be a common activity, particularly during miners' strikes when the coal was used for cooking and heating, keeping struggling families alive.

Our path joined a road running above Collywell Bay. At the end of the bay, on the left hand side, is an octagonal building, The Revenue House, where a check was kept on ships entering and leaving Seaton Sluice Harbour. This is where the Seaton Burn makes its modest exit from the land, its waters flowing under a road bridge, through sand blackened by coal dust, to join the North Sea. This used to be a busy port. Ships transported local coal from here down the east coast to London.

The Revenue House

The entrance to the harbour is protected from the ravages of the North Sea by a pier of rocks built by Ralph Delaval, but there were problems. A dangerous bend in the channel meant that ships had to wait off shore for favourable winds before entering harbour. The Seaton Burn was also prone to silting up with sand washed in by the tide. Ralph Delaval built a sluice designed to retain water during an outgoing tide. When the sluice was opened a head of water rushed out to sea taking the sand along with it.

This device gave the community its unique name of Seaton Sluice.

Now it was low tide and craft in the harbour were lying tilted on their sides, moored on the coaly rocks below. We tried to imagine the comings and goings of this busy little port during the eighteenth century. We walked towards a white pub standing above a bend in the harbour. Here a footbridge led across a deep cut in the rocks. This cut was blasted through by John and Thomas Delaval in 1761 to create a more reliable entrance to the harbour. We stood on the bridge, looking down at the deep black water below us. The channel, 52 feet deep, 900 feet long and 30 feet wide, was quite a feat of engineering. When it was officially opened, John Delaval declared a holiday and free beer for all was served in local pubs. The Delavals appear to have been good landlords and were proud of being able to provide employment for the area. Owners of a brewery, a quarry and a shipyard as well as the mines and glassworks, their influence on the local community was extensive. They lived in Seaton Delaval Hall, a magnificent building designed by Vanburgh, a mile up the A190, known locally as 'The Avenue'.

We sat on a seat near the cut to eat our sandwiches, looking out to white sweeping waves breaking on the beach beyond the harbour entrance. I took the opportunity to examine my left foot which had started to hurt. With dismay I discovered the start of a blister on my second toe. A blister…. I never had blisters…a blister on my first day…what bad luck. We tried to pad it with tissues to stop any more friction and went on, down to the beach bordered by white sand dunes.

I remember walking here from Whitley Bay with Mum and Dad and my brother David. I was fourteen and wearing a new navy and white spotted sundress bought from a catalogue. I really fancied myself wearing that and posed lying in the sand dunes waiting for Mr. Right to come along as he always did in the Doris Day movies of the fifties. But the top kept slipping, revealing too much of my developing upper body, and chilly northern temperatures sadly made the dress utterly unsuitable.

The beach is well known to us as we used to do a beach patrol for the R.S.P.B. Our task was to search for oiled seabirds, to note their species and the extent of the damage.
Our specimens were usually dead and had to be buried so that they wouldn't be washed up on future occasions.
One of our patrols took place after a known oil spillage. The devastation was widespread. Birds lay blackened like lumps of sludge. Our undertaker's role seemed to be never ending and we resorted to mass graves. Thankfully there was no such gruesome task to be faced today, just a walk along the beach towards our next landmark - Blyth harbour and its wind-farm.

Seaton Sluice

Tide wriggles out.
Reflections waver
Ropes recoil
Boats keel over
Coal cakes sand banks
Light refracts
Birds march in ranks.
Tide's wriggled out.

It was always a source of amazement to us that the landscape of the beach changed dramatically with the tides. Streams which ran down the beach to the sea changed their path every month. Sometimes they flowed in deep channels and were difficult to cross, at other times they spread themselves into a shallow shawl of glistening water which we walked through without any trouble. There were huge concrete sea defences left from the war years which were sometimes non-existent, sometimes just stepping stones in the sand and occasionally like a concrete city, higher than a man.

These sandy beaches along the coast from Whitley Bay to Blyth were the Spanish Costas of my childhood. Unfortunately nobody bothered to tell the weatherman so many of my memories involve coming out of the invariably perishingly cold North Sea and shivering like a jelly until a very brisk towelling off restored a little circulation. The only likeness to Spain was that my chattering teeth probably sounded like castanets! Not that I ever swam in the North Sea. I tried, but it took forty-odd years and the much warmer waters of the Andaman Sea off the Coast of Thailand before I could claim even a minimal ability at staying afloat in water. The weather couldn't have been so terrible though because I also remember that hundreds of people used to flock to the coast in the summer. During the local miners' holidays or in Scots' week, when the total population of Glasgow, or so it seemed, decamped to Whitley Bay, there could be so many people on the beach that it was difficult to find a few square feet of sand to call your own. Mind you there was always plenty of sand about when it came to eating your boiled egg sandwiches. I can still feel the gritty texture between my teeth. On this chilly June day we had the place pretty much to ourselves.

As we walked along the promenade at Blyth, close to where the Jubilee café used to be, I remembered a time when I was about eight or nine years old. I was walking the same stretch of promenade with my father when, about twenty yards away across the beach, we spotted my cousin John and Uncle Jack. They were busy building sand castles, Uncle Jack kneeling on the sand and John, who is about two years younger than me, as we say in this area, on his "honkers", i.e. sitting on his heels. I ran down the steps from the promenade, across the beach, put my foot under John's behind and promptly tipped him on his face. Both John and Uncle Jack looked round, surprised but not so surprised as I was when I realised that these two figures were not John and Uncle Jack. In fact, face to face, these two total strangers bore them no resemblance whatsoever. Now, some fifty years on I could smile as I remembered my spluttering embarrassment and speedy retreat back to the promenade. H

We walked on towards our landmark, the nine giant turbines standing sentinel on Blyth North Pier. They produce electricity at wind speeds between 10 and 60 miles per hour. Full output is reached at 26 miles per hour. The project was started in 1992 by Border Wind when the turbines were shipped from Antwerp and installed on the pier foundations which had already been prepared.

Blyth Wind-Farm

A second phase of two turbines, commissioned in 2000, was to be the country's first offshore wind farm. Effects on the environment were a concern, so a local ornithologist was employed to monitor deaths of birds flying into the turning blades. He walks the beach twice a week noting species and the nature of casualties.

Towards the end of the beach a short stretch of promenade fronts what used to be a pleasure area for Blyth. Here we left the sea and took to the road for a few yards in order to access the port of Blyth through gates near the storage sheds. Blyth used to be an important industrial town, the fourth coal shipping port in the country and a centre for ship - building. Trucks pulled by horses ran on wooden rails transporting coal from Bebside Colliery down to the river. Local historians like to claim this as the first railway in Britain. Colliers, moored at wooden staiths, were waiting to take their cargo of coal to ports along the coast. Blyth Harbour was wide and had deep water so ships up to five hundred feet long could berth there. Ships in dry dock towered over the houses. After the shipyards and pits closed, Blyth's importance as an industrial town faded and the staiths became derelict. Recently, however, Blyth Renaissance Partnership was formed and the whole waterfront area has been re-developed. The staiths have been clad with new decking, creating a smart recreation area and the Council plan to commission sculptures to complete the project. Trade is being attracted to the port. Four ships make a triangular journey between the Baltic, Rotterdam and Blyth. Wood pulp and alumina are being imported and timber from Keilder Forest is surprisingly, being exported to Finland. Aluminium is shipped to Germany and opencast coal to Norway.

Beyond the port we passed through the pleasant surroundings of Ridley Park, named after Viscount Matthew White Ridley who is considered to be the founder of modern Blyth. He instigated a programme of dredging so that larger vessels could berth in the harbour. He also gave land to be used for the building of a mechanics' institute, a church and a hospital. A true benefactor.

On the other side of the Park, just outside his office which used to be the Blyth mortuary, we met John Craigs, the Port Health Officer, an ex work colleague of Harry's. After initial greetings we told John what we were doing and about our problem with the River Blyth. 'Well I'm just about finished here,' he said, 'If you don't mind waiting while I polish off some paper work I'll run you round to Cambois.' I quickly decided that in this situation practicalities must come before niceties and gave in gracefully, saying we certainly didn't mind waiting. John's wife, Linda, also turned up having timed her shopping expedition to coincide with his finishing time. We took the opportunity for a rest whilst enjoying a coffee, a chat and a game of football with their dog.

When he had finished, John took us round for the next leg of our journey to Newbiggin. He dropped us off at North Blyth where colliers used to dock. Here is a network of old staiths lapped by black water. Three red hoppers, which store alumina, are linked to Alcan's smelter by a rail line which runs behind a high safety fence. There is a constant background humming sound from the wind turbines. A little way inland is Blyth Power Station built in the 1950s to meet an increase in demand for electricity, its four tall chimneys dominating the area. A few terraced houses remain in this industrial landscape, almost cut off from the rest of civilisation - this is Cambois.

As a youngster at school in Blyth, Cambois (pronounced Cammus) was a place of some mystery. It was very close to Blyth, only the width of the river away, and yet I had never been there, didn't know anybody who lived there and indeed wondered whether it really existed because people also spoke of North Blyth being across the river and there hardly seemed room for two communities.

My first experience of the place was as a sixteen-year-old playing football for Cramlington Juniors. It seemed that whenever we had an away game to somewhere like Cambois (was there anywhere like Cambois?) rumours of the perils of the fixture abounded. Some teams were reputedly "dirty"-"you'll be lucky to come away with two legs never mind two points"-it was two points for a win in those days. Others lacked facilities - "you'll have to get changed behind a hedge" -sometimes that was not far from the truth. In the case of Cambois it was the spectators. I happened to play on the left wing for Cramlington. "You're playing outside left at Cambois." Eyes twinkled, grins widened, voices adopted a note of incredulity as though I had just announced that I was off to play in Timbuktu but expected to be back in time for tea. "You're in for a rare afternoon. You see the spectators are nearly all women and they're stone mad. When you're running down the wing they stick their umbrellas between your legs and trip you up or else they just whack you with them or stick them in you as you go past." My self confidence took another knock when I ran out onto the field and discovered that a lot of the spectators along the touchline were indeed women and some of them had umbrellas. It was a little while before I realised that although they made a lot of noise their bark was worse than their bite. ℋ

We found an underpass which took us beneath the railway line and down to the beach. Here was my first major surprise of our walk. I had expected Cambois beach to be marred by industrial debris or sea washed coal. Instead a broad, untrodden swathe of golden sand stretched out in front of us. We searched the skyline and found our next objective - St. Bartholomew's Church at Newbiggin, a pale edifice in the distance, a ghostly tower and spire against dark clouds. It looked diminutive. We still had a long way to go. We reached

what is known as Seaton Point and a fast flowing channel of water, the River Wansbeck, barred our way. We weren't sure just how deep it was so we turned towards the land. At the point, the road did a nose dive down to the river. There, two locals were exchanging stories, leaning against an upturned boat.

'Hello…We're looking for some local knowledge. Is it possible to walk across the Wansbeck?'

'What are ye planning to de like? Yer not called Jesus or anything are ye? Yer not planning to do summat daft? Cos there's 30,000 folks been drowned here.' The heavily built man turned from his boat to eye us up and down as if to see if we were in our right minds.

'Aye there's all sorts of currents,' his companion agreed.

Assured of an audience, the big man continued.

'This is the worst bit of coast in the country fer drownin, folks haven't got a clue. Like that lot across there…', he said pointing to the caravan site on the other bank of the river. 'Yer knaa them red things what ye throw to somebody in the watter?' He indicated the posts where life belts should have been hanging. 'They pinch them.' And his chin came down onto his chest in a nod of righteous indignation. 'They think they're boolies.' We assumed he meant tyres or girds, something to be bowled. 'And there's a bloke comes down and pinches the rope on that one.' He pointed to a life belt post on this side of the river. 'He does it time and again. Says

it isn't him. But one time he left his knife.' He nodded sagely.
'We're walking up the coast. Is it possible to paddle across?' we asked.
'Oh…ye just want a paddle?
'No they're walkin' up the coast man.'
'Oh well you can plodge across. It might be quite deep like. Why don't you walk up to the bridge and down t'other side?'
The road bridge a little way off carried the busy A 189 so we were trying to avoid it.
' How far ye walkin like?'
'From Tyne to Tweed.'
'Ah that'll be a nice walk. There's some lovely bits of coast,' his marra, his friend, said appreciatively.
'There's that other river. The…'
'The Aln?'
'No man. The Lyne…They've got to cross the Lyne. There was a bloke drowned wiv his horse and cart in the Lyne. Found him on the bank.' We thanked them and left, ruminating over drowned lost souls and headed towards the A189. Discretion was the better part of valour.
We hadn't gone far when we met three men out walking, 'Last of the Summer Wine' style. They were peering through field glasses.
'Anything interesting?' we asked.
'Only skylarks,' was their reply.
'Skylarks aren't 'only' these days though are they? They're getting to be a rarity,' we commented. They murmured agreement. 'Having a good day?' we enquired. They told us where they had come from and we told them what we were doing.
'Oh you'll have to cross the Lyne. If it's low tide you will be able to scramble under the pipe. I like it. It's interesting,' said the sun reddened man with his sweater tied round his waist. 'And then there are the gypsies.' He was obviously relishing old traditions and local knowledge. We bade them good day and wondered about this crossing of the Lyne. In these parts it seemed to hold more significance than crossing the equator. Our path took us under the busy spine road and continued along the riverbank but we needed to cross the river and loop back on the other side. What had seemed to be a footbridge turned out to be a Water Board gantry marked as private property but it was easily accessible so we trespassed and got across. We suspected we were not the first to do so. A path on the north bank of the Wansbeck led us up to Sandy Bay Caravan Site, then on to some allotments on the outskirts of Newbiggin. My feet were tired and sore so I paused to look at the rows of neatly planted vegetables punctuated by ramshackle sheds and greenhouses.
'Do ye like gardening then?' came a question from among the foliage.
'Yes…yes I like gardening,' I replied taken aback at the directness of the question.

'Aye…My missus is into soaps. Can't abide them so I come and amuse myself gardening.

I grew some of that…ye know…like the song…Auf Wiedersehen…200 plants. I didn't know what to do with 'em. Used to grow five different kinds of tomatoes. It was too much. I had to give some away. Then they expect it. Following year they were all saying, 'Where's me tomatoes?" and he shrugged philosophically. Changing tack he said, 'I take the missus dancing every Wednesday.'

'Ballroom dancing?'

'Oh yes. I can tango you know. I can do it now George Raft's dead. I don't have to be afraid of overshadowing him. I used to do the quick step till they slapped a speed limit on the floor. I had five grocery shops in North Shields before I retired. Then we went to live in Whitley Bay and I worked at St. Mary's…the Lighthouse. I used to have a string fastened to me big toe and when I jerked it, it pulled a blind down. Well how do you think the light flashed?' Reeling from Geordie humour and tales of his accomplishments, I bade him good day and made to catch up with Harry.

We were now approaching the promenade at Newbiggin, footsore and weary but with a feeling of achievement that our first day had been accomplished. We found our B&B tucked away up a side street. It was an ordinary nineteen fifties semi. We rang the bell and were greeted by Mary Dodds.

'Oh. Hello. Come in. I'm Mary and you are?'

'Kath and Harry.'

'Kathy and Harry.' It was all very familiar with Mary and everybody was spoken of by their first name.

She is a lady devoted to her B&B. 'Oh I'm always busy aren't I Bob?' Bob nodded. 'I like to do jobs straight away you know Kathy. I get the washing done in the morning and then bake a few scones. While the scones are baking I do some ironing. And then there's my sewing. I like my sewing. I made some old fashioned aprons for a fête for my daughter-in-law. She sent me a photograph of a woman wearing one and being introduced to Prince Charles.'

'Oh so you could add 'By Royal Appointment' to your brochure,' I said.

Mary smiled. 'And we have guests from all over the world. Czechoslovakia, Finland, America.' As if to prove it she produced a post card from Czechoslovakia. 'Yes, well its nice to keep in touch.'

We were regaled with stories of Mary's family, all of them being spoken of by their Christian names and we had to piece their relationships together like a jigsaw puzzle. Mary's house was super clean. Her oven door shone and reflected like a mirror. There were plastic flowers everywhere, nylon pillow slips and hidden toilet rolls. Bob, her husband, took a back seat where the B&B was concerned, he just observed all in silent amusement.

We enjoyed a welcome cup of tea, chicken sandwiches and a piece of orange cake. It was all delicious and most unexpected. On Mary's recommendation we went to the Old Ship for our evening meal. It was pleasantly seedy with a few locals eating and watching T.V. on a giant screen. There were photos of sports teams; cricket, tennis, and rugby. Harry chose the Old Ship mixed grill. He remarked that they were trying to solve the problems of the meat market single-handed. He had a pork chop, a lamb chop, lambs liver, steak, 2 sausages, mushrooms, black pudding, onion rings, chips and salad all for £4-20.

Afterwards we went onto the 'prom' and watched the sea bursting over the new sea wall. It wasn't a particularly rough night but we were reminded that Newbiggin lives with the sea as a constant neighbour and provider. Many of the houses still have boats drawn up in their gardens. Like many places on this coast, Newbiggin has not been immune from marine disasters. A framed report on Bob and Mary's wall told that, 'On 9th Dec 1904, 'The Anglia' went aground off the Needles Eye. Eight men went out to rescue 'The Anglia' and the lifeboat crew also went out. There was one survivor. The dead were buried on Sunday 11th, a cold day and it is recorded that 20,000 attended the service.' Perhaps some of this story is apocryphal but the dangers are real and experienced by many locals. I was reminded of paintings by the Cullercoats artists showing women strong and brave, sleeves rolled up, hair blown by the wind, hauling on ropes to pull wrecked boats ashore. Perhaps Grace Darling's heroic rescue was not so out of character with women of our North Sea coast.

It had been a long day so when we returned to Bob and Mary's we avoided getting involved in conversation. We went straight to bed and were soon lost in a deep sleep.

Day 2
Newbiggin-by-the-Sea
to
Warkworth

We had breakfast in the conservatory. Other guests were Audrey and Don from Carlisle. They were in Newbiggin to attend the funeral of a friend. One of the family came to collect them after breakfast for a 9-15 a.m. service at St. Bartholomew's on the cliffs.

We called at the chemists to buy toe guards to protect my blistered toe. We also bought some fruit for our picnic lunch. I found a seat on the prom, and prepared to do a repair job on my feet. As I peeled back my sock, two fellows passing by said: 'Wondered what the smell was!' Cheeky! I hurried on to catch up with Harry. Passing the lifeboat station, we continued to the end of the promenade where metal bollards were topped with figures of shiny black puffins with bright orange striped beaks. They looked cheerful and seemed to be wishing us well for the day ahead.

Newbiggin Bay is sheltered by rocky headlands. St.Bartholomew's Church stands alone above the bay, a clear landmark to those at sea. Its tower dates from the 13th.

century and the spire was added a hundred years later. Looking at this sheltered bay, deserted except for a few dog walkers, it is hard to picture it as it used to be, a busy port with as many foreign ships as English in its harbour. Indeed Newbiggin used to rival Newcastle as the busiest port in the North East. There was a pier just below the church and in the 18th century, the town had granaries, shops and inns. Along the edge of the bay were upturned boats used as houses by fishermen. To keep their fish fresh, they stored their catch in trays lined with grass from the church yard. They believed that, as it had come from consecrated ground, the grass should provide them with added good fortune. The vicar tried to levy tythes on the population but they objected. To bring them to heel, the vicar refused to attend worship at St. Bartholomew's and the building fell into disrepair. In 1908 colliery shafts were sunk and the town expanded to house miners employed in the pits.

We took a few minutes to look into the churchyard and found graves of inhabitants who had died at sea or been killed in the mines. Gravestones were pitted and weathered by wind and salt spray. John Brown, Coxswain of the lifeboat crew....his son aged 14...John Lipton whose ship was wrecked in a 'tremendous tumult' at Cresswell.... Life had been hard here on the North East coast. Those who slumber in the cemetery are rocked by the constant sound of the sea breaking on the shores below.

St. Bartholomew's Church

A witness,
Solitary in grief
Mourns the long dead of the town.
The wind removes our tributes to the drowned
Forming strange hieroglyphics in the stone.
Sand on sandstone grinds them down,
Ashes to ashes, sand to sand,
Tombstones erased – Lives expunged.
Gone are their doings
Gone to sand.

North easterly winds moan as they sweep through the aisles of gravestones and two corbel heads, worn into eyeless effigies, peer out from either side of the porch, searching far horizons. Nothing stands between the churchyard and the sea and the clear windows of the church bring its presence right into daily worship.

Humbled by these thoughts of human mortality, we walked silently along the cliff path through the caravan site and along 'the moor'. Our next objective was Alcan's Smelter which dominated the skyline. Golfers were out on the links beside us. We looked at eiders - Cuddy's Ducks - offshore and then spotted a seal basking on the rocks. Harry went down to take its photograph. He inched closer and closer, then it became nervous, turned tail and flopped into the sea never to be seen again. Another photographic gem lost to posterity!

Rain threatened so we put on waterproofs and continued, picking our way through waste debris floating on a stagnant inlet of water below Alcan Power Station. We reached the road where the sun came out and we peeled off the waterproofs again observed by passing lorry drivers who gave us a toot on their horn in appreciation of this public strip-tease.

Adjacent to the smelter is Ellington Colliery, the last deep mine in Northumberland. Some time ago it was threatened with closure but was rescued by R.J.Budge. Coal seams stretch for miles under the sea. Inland is Woodhorn Colliery which has been preserved as a museum. Here there are rooms set out as miners' houses used to be in the early 20th century with clippy mats, tin baths and black-leaded kitchen ranges. There is also an exhibition of paintings, the work of miners in their hard won leisure time.

We walked on to Lynemouth and, joy of joys, found a chemist who sold blister treatments. They could offer some relief for the days to come.

The tide was well in so we crossed the River Lyne by the road. Looking down at its green, deep channel we were rather glad we didn't attempt the gyrations of crawling under the pipe or wading across. I began to give more credence to the tales of those two locals. On the beach I saw the remnants of Northumberland's coaly past, stretches of sand blackened by coal dust. In places the black shale was spread out like the lacy patterns of a shawl. The dunes were a wasteland of rubbish and spoil heaps. Travellers were encamped close to the Lyne and their ponies grazed, tethered on small pockets of grass.

Tethered Ponies

Further on, one of the travellers passed us by, his legs swinging over the edge of his horse-drawn cart. 'Hello better morning,' he said to Harry. And then to me, 'Hello better morning.'
'A somewhat limited range of conversation,' joked Harry.

Twelve thirty and we were at Cresswell. It had been a long morning and we felt as though time had been wasted but we weren't sure how. We approached a general dealer's with picnic tables out in the sun. A tempting notice made us stop and change our lunchtime plans from cheese sandwiches to hot pasties. We sat at a picnic table outside the shop munching happily. Across the fields we could see an ancient peel tower amongst trees. This was home to the Cresswell family. It was from here that the White Lady of Cresswell saw her Danish lover murdered by her brothers. In her anguish she starved herself to death. Well we wouldn't starve, the pasties were delicious. After we had finished I went into the shop to make some enquiries. A young, dark haired girl asked if she could help.

'I've read in a guidebook that there is a sunken oak forest somewhere on the beach near here,' I said.

She puffed out her face, leaned on the counter and looked utterly defeated. Then as inspiration dawned, she shouted through to the back sitting room, 'Brenda…Brenda!'

Brenda emerged through the door. 'There's a woman wants to ask you something.'

'I've read that there is a sunken oak forest on the beach near here. Could you tell me how to find it?'

'Oh..yes. We've quite a stretch of forest all along the coast but you can best see it where the dunes start.' She led us out of the shop and indicated a track leading to the beach. 'Go down there and walk along the sea defences. When they end and the dunes begin…well you're walking on it. It's like clay and you can see wood inside. When it's low tide you can walk out to the end of the rocks and look into the sea. There are remains there too but be careful because the incoming tide swirls round the rocks and you can get cut off.'

We thanked her and made off towards the track. Down on the beach the large concrete defence blocks were easily visible. They ended and the dunes began. We looked down and saw what seemed to be a compressed mass of cork-like substance. Embedded were recognisable pieces of wood. Flakes of bark could also be identified. Under this layer of wood a band of conglomerate, clay combined with pebbles, disappeared into the sand. Evidence of a changing tide line from times past.

We left Cresswell behind and headed on to Druridge Bay, a long sweep of golden sand backed by white dunes. We were going to appreciate just how long that sweep of sand was in actuality. Away in the far distance was Coquet Island, close to our night's destination in Warkworth. A clutch of trees, dark on the horizon, marked Hauxley Nature Reserve. We walked and walked. It was warm and sunny. An enjoyable afternoon. At one time land bordering this section of coast was laid waste to open-cast mine workings and 'Big Geordie',

a giant land excavator, worked incessantly gnawing great chasms out of the land. Grey shale spoil heaps marred the landscape. Not now, there was no visible sign of what had gone before. The area has been landscaped and made into a country park with visitor centre, water sports area and pleasant paths circling hills and lakeside. Quite a transformation.

At about three fifteen we headed into the dunes to cross a streamlet and sat down for a rest. An elderly man passed us wheeling a bike. We talked about our destination. 'Rather you than me. Quarter of an hour and I'll be home at Red Row supping a cup of coffee. Looks as though you're going to get wet.' And he wheeled on. We looked up and indeed saw black clouds above. We staggered to our feet and out of the shelter of the dunes, discovering a different day. It was spitting with rain and very cold. We got the waterproofs out and were glad of their warmth though the rain soon stopped. As we reached the top sweep of the bay, Coquet Island disappeared behind the headland and with nothing left as our focus, we trudged on becoming tired. Had we begun to fantasise? Were the empty ocean and endless vistas of sand getting to us? We began putting our own words to well known songs.

'How far is it to Coquet Isle
Is it too far?
Will we find a lighthouse there?
Lit by a star?
Will we find a publican?
Is he within?
Can we shout across the bar?
Two tonics please with gin.'

In the distance we caught sight of a figure striding towards us on the beach. We obviously were hallucinating, it was Father Christmas. The figure had a shock of white curly hair and a matching luxuriant beard but alas no red cape, just a much worn sweater and some green wellies. Brian Little, a local ornithologist, greeted us, smiling and narrowing his eyes. 'Well Hello,' he said, 'Didn't expect to bump into you here.'
Brian is an old friend of mine from years back. We explained our journey.
'Well you've made it to Hauxley anyhow.'
'This is where Brian has his ringing station,' I explained to Harry.
'Yes, between our wood and the Northumberland Wildlife Trust's Reserve next door, it's a great area for attracting migrants. The reserve has a salt water lake and islands. They're going to build a new reception centre with lottery money. Should be very smart.'
Brian was walking ahead through Hauxley village towards a wood.

'We ring birds and track their movements round the world. Forty years, forty years since Bryan Galloway and I stumbled into Hauxley Wood. We knew instantly that it was a perfect spot for a ringing station. The coast swings right out to sea and Coquet Island, off shore, attracts migrating birds.'
'That's why the island seemed to disappear,' I thought.
'The wood is perfect cover for a bird tired after its long migration flight so it comes down to rest. Francis Widdrington owned the wood, it had been planted by his grandfather and he was delighted to put it to good use as it were. Come and see our Heligoland trap,' and without more ado Brian strode off up a track and into a clutch of trees. 'We put this up on a bitterly cold winter's day in 1963.' We looked at the large structure of wood and netting and wondered how it worked. 'It's like a funnel. We fan out through the wood making a noise and the birds fly through the bushes in front of us and eventually into the wide part of the trap. They fly on, gradually being forced down to the narrowest part and into a catching area. We ring them and record the species. Ring numbers are sent to the British Museum. Anyone finding a dead ringed bird returns the ring. This is our headquarters,' and he indicated a hut in the wood, 'donated by Derek Crouch.'
He was responsible for opencast mine workings at Widdrington. 'Do you want to doss down for the night?' Brian asked.

'Thanks. That's kind but we're booked into a B&B in Warkworth so we'd better press on.

'Well come back sometime and I'll show you the trap in action…could do some mist netting as well.'

'O.K. we'll do that.'

'Have a brew before you go on.'

I looked at Harry. Did we really have time? 'Alright, just a quick one.'

Brian disappeared into the hut and we sat down on the plastic chairs. He continued to talk from inside. Nothing stopped Brian once he was in full flow.

'I was in Antartica last Autumn. It was amazing..the wildlife. It was a cruise on a Russian ship. That Russian captain…such a big character, brave..but it was nearly a tragedy.' Brian loved telling stories and we were hooked.

'Why? What happened?' He came outside with steaming mugs of tea.

'We were due to go ashore in the zodiacs to an island. I didn't like the look of some storm clouds boiling up so I decided to stay on board. There was another man who missed the trip. He'd slept in. He was glad later on. The party had just landed and one zodiac was heading back to the ship when the wind got up. Waves twice the height of the ship. You know, I must have a guardian angel. The bosun was stuck at sea in the zodiac. He was lying down spread-eagled, clinging onto the ropes on either side. He couldn't get back to shore. He was there for forty minutes and then he shouted, 'Captain, I can't hold on any more.' The captain decided the ship would have to move. So they shot a rope across to the bosun and hauled the zodiac back and got him aboard in a breeches buoy but it was touch and go. The ship went round the island with mountainous waves…I'm a good sailor…never sea sick, thank god. Well, the party that had gone ashore, some of them were just in tee shirts under their wet suits. They had to spend the night under the zodiac. Amazing we didn't have a death…The crew managed to get them back on board next morning. I was helping them. 'Get your clothes off and get into bed. Cuddle each other,' and he giggled. 'One old couple refused.'

'It's years since we did that and we're not going to do it now.'

'Cuddle each other or you'll die,' I said. 'You've got to get warm. Yes, we were lucky there were no lives lost. It could have been me and with my diabetes…Someone up there's watching out for me…my guardian angel.'

We said our goodbyes. We'd enjoyed our brief respite talking to Brian but now pressed on along the minor road towards Amble. An inviting finger post pointed through the fields to High Hauxley and Amble but we thought better of it and continued along the road with the spire of Amble cemetery getting closer. A flock of goldfinches flew from branch to branch, embroidering the air with threads of gold. Coquet light was now visible and our steps quickened as we hit the streets of the town.

Amble used to be a dilapidated port on the estuary of the River Coquet but has recently undergone a facelift thanks to an interested and active community and local organisations like the Harbour Commission, One North East, Northumbrian Water and the RNLI who have all invested money in Amble's revitalisation. The estuary has been dredged and the pier and quays have been repaired and made safe so that visitors can now enjoy a walk beside the water. Many of the fishing boats working out of Amble harbour have young skippers and crews and they proudly claim that Amble is the best port in Northumberland.

We made our way through the streets of the town and returned to the river outside the marina where we decided we needed an extra perk and shared a Mars bar. Warkworth Castle lay ahead dominating the estuary. A girl wearing an orange shirt and setting a cracking pace, sprinted past us. 'Keep sight of her, she might know a short cut by the river.' But our weary feet were much too slow and she soon disappeared from view. We were into Warkworth before any short cut presented itself but decided to go down past The Sun Inn. It did cut a corner off and we were soon passing beneath an ancient guardhouse, onto the narrow, stone, 14th century bridge over the Coquet and uphill, heading for

North Cottage, home of Edith and John Howliston. They are the prime movers of Warkworth in bloom competition. Gardens of Warkworth are open to visitors on a day in July each year.

'Oh Warkworth in bloom is no problem It's Britain in Bloom that we'd like to win,' said Edith.

Their garden is planned in a series of terraces leading steeply up from the main road. A fishpond full of carp is crossed by a slate bridge and a path leads round to the back of the house where we were greeted warmly. 'Oh, you look tired. Come in. There'll be a cup of tea for you in the lounge. This is your room. Just come in when you're ready.'

I peeled off my trainers and gingerly put my feet down to the floor. A sharp pain shot upwards. Carefully I inched back the socks to reveal an enormous bleb of a blister covering my entire right heel. The original blister between my toes was still there, only bigger. My heart sank. Would I be able to go on next day? Anyway first things first, a cup of tea, a shower and a meal.

The other guest at North Cottage was Brian who was in Warkworth to re-visit old haunts. He intended to go to Amble Cemetery to find the grave of a friend who had introduced him to Northumberland after the Second World

Castle Street - Warkworth

expensive meal. Feeling a little refreshed we slowly returned to Castle Street. Art Galleries and gift shops were now closed. Warkworth Castle, floodlit, stood proudly atop its green mound which in spring is covered with daffodils. There has been a castle here since 1139 but existing remains date from 1332 when the castle came into the hands of Percy, Earl of Northumberland. Alnwick, the other Northumbrian castle belonging to the Percys, was used as a fortress and Warkworth became their fortified manor house. Three scenes of Shakespeare's Henry lV are set in Warkworth Castle.

We gabbled on about blisters and walking up the Northumberland Coast only to learn later that Brian was a double amputee and had lost his legs as a result of smoking. Blisters paled into insignificance. Edith recommended two places for our evening meal, 'The Hermitage' and 'Topsy Turvey', the latter being a bit more expensive. We decided to go to the Hermitage feeling almost too tired to do justice to an

We relaxed over a glass of wine, and having decided that part of our shivery, tired feeling might be due to de-hydration, drank umpteen glasses of water. We slowly began to feel more normal.

Before we returned to North Cottage, we strolled down past the sandstone church with its twisted mediaeval spire. It has a fine Norman nave, nearly thirty yards long but its oldest treasure is a Saxon gravestone to be found in a recess in the south wall. We continued along a path beside the River Coquet. It was so peaceful. Only jumping fish catching flies broke the silence. No wonder a hermit chose to settle near a cave further up river. Thomas Barker was appointed in 1487 by the Earl of Northumberland to pray for souls of noble men. George Lancaster, a later hermit, in return for his religious duties, received pasture for his cattle, two loads of wood and a draught of fish every Sunday. It is possible to walk along the river and visit the remains of the hermitage, a stone built hall, a tiny chapel and a sacristy, but we had done enough walking for the day and turned back, looking up at the turrets and towers of Warkworth Castle on their lofty position above us.

The River Coquet and Warkworth Castle

The Church of St. Lawrence - Warkworth

There has been a church on this site since 737 A.D. but the building we see today dates from 1132. Previous churches were destroyed by Viking raiders. The church was designed, not only as a place of worship but also as a sanctuary, a place of safety for the people of the area. Its walls are thick and strong and the original windows were high and narrow

**Day 3
Warkworth
to Craster**

Next morning Harry did an expert job creating padding around the blister on my heel and once I had carefully positioned my foot in its trainer, I found the pain was about bearable. We discovered that Edith had been up since five o'clock working in the garden. 'Well it's the only time you get any peace. There are no phone calls at that time in the morning. Sometimes I get up at three when the birds start singing.'

That's what I call dedication. A woman with a mission in life. But her enthusiasm for gardening did not stop at her own front patch.

'We've made a millennium garden down near the bridge. We had it all planted out but the council came round and sprayed it with weed killer. Well you can't say too much because we're usually at them to spray round the village. We've got a seat for the garden which needs fixing in. John did the last one and it looks as though he'll have to do it again. If you can do something people are always coming to you. He gets landed with everything. He's putting tables out for tonight's fund raising for Warkworth in Bloom. We're having wine and savouries.'

Just then the post arrived and we could hear John and Edith ooh-ing and aah-ing over some pictures. Edith soon came through to show us a handful of photographs.

'We had an American staying with us. He tagged along with us to everything. Here we are at the garden centre buying bedding plants. John is my tea ready?' and she settled herself to tell us more. Gone was our early start.

'You've got to have a sense of humour in this job,' she said. 'You meet all types and some think they can trample all over in their muddy boots. One German couple brought their own sausages and kept them in the fridge. They cut a slice off each day to take with them. Are you just going to walk up the road to Alnmouth?' she asked.

'No we want to walk along the dunes. Should we go down to the bridge and take the path?'

'No, go through our field, turn left along the lane. It brings you out on the road a little further up but you are only on it for a short while. Take the next turning on the right and the track will lead you down to the beach.'

Her directions were true enough and we were soon enjoying the morning sunshine and a very pleasant walk among white sand dunes, taking delight in finding numerous wild flowers; ladies bedstraw, thrift, cranesbill, vipers bugloss. In the bright morning light, Coquet Island, a mile out to sea from the mouth of the river, seemed much closer than it had last night.

Alnmouth

Sinuous River Aln
Reluctantly meanders seawards,
Lingering lovingly
In lazy loops.
Above its banks
The red roofed cheerful town
Climbs up to catch the cry of gulls.

Kathleen Colbert

43

It is a low lying, windswept island a quarter of a mile long. Little grows there but grass and ragwort. Its prominent feature is an 80 foot high lighthouse. Before it was built, a boat called the 'Catherine' from Sunderland went aground. Nine men clung to the rigging all night but people from Amble were unable to save them because they did not have a lifeboat. All nine men drowned. Built into the lighthouse cottage are the remains of a chapel and a priests' cell, once occupied by hermits looking for a solitary life. The lighthouse is a good marker for migratory birds who landfall here after their long flights. The island holds about 90% of the UK's breeding population of roseate terns. Thousands of other seabirds nest there each summer including puffins and eider ducks, this being the eider's most southerly nesting place. White angora rabbits were introduced to the island but it was soon overrun and they had to be destroyed.

We came to the estuary of the Aln and were surrounded by a tide of sea pink in the adjacent marshland. We followed a path towards some cottages knowing that we had to re-join the busy road to cross the Aln and make our way into Alnmouth. We stopped at Saw Mill Cottage to ask directions of the owner then turned to photograph Alnmouth and the estuary. Just as we were finishing, the man reappeared saying, 'We've just made a pot of tea. Would you like a cup?'

We gratefully accepted and followed him round to the back garden of their weekend cottage. His wife and two grandsons made us welcome and we sat down in their cottage garden enjoying a period of warm sunshine. Our conversation turned to where we were from and we discovered they were from Gosforth.
'I used to teach in Gosforth,' I volunteered, 'At Gosforth East Middle School.'
'Oh, my cousin was Head of Gosforth Park First School, Jim Standish.'
'Oh yes I know Jim.'
'She might know…'said his wife.
'Oh no she's far too young'
'I liked the Head, at the East.. Mac…something?' she continued.
'MacAndrews. Yes, I liked Mac very much' I responded. 'I taught at Gosforth East for a long time before I became head of Throckley Middle School. Which school do you go to?' I enquired, turning to the eldest grandson.
'Gosforth Central Middle School.'
'Oh, yes. We know your headteacher, Mrs. Darwin, very well'
'James took part in a Middle School celebration last night,' said his proud Grandma. 'He recited a poem which he had written.'

'Oh that's excellent. What was the poem about?' James became very bashful and muttered something about his wishes and dreams.

'You know I think Middle Schools do a very good job. It's a pity there are so few of them,' said Grandad.

'In Newcastle there are only nine Middle Schools. Because they exist alongside the two-tier system and often feel under threat, the Headteachers work very closely together. That's how I came to be friendly with Mrs. Darwin.' And so the conversation went on. It was so pleasant sitting there in the sunshine that we almost lost sight of our objective, however Grandad offered to give us a lift into Alnmouth. He was going to buy fish and chips as a treat for the boys' lunch. Having dallied for such a long time we felt we had an excuse for accepting a lift so we gratefully said 'yes' and set off for Alnmouth. On the way, Grandad pointed out a house with a number of garden ornaments. No they weren't gnomes. Far grander than that. One was a replica of the Statue of Liberty! Grandad drove towards the bridge and we glimpsed the snaking River Aln making its way to the sea at the foot of red roofed houses, part of this charming seaside town. Passengers on London - Edinburgh trains are treated to this tantalising view as they speed northward to Scotland. John Wesley described Alnmouth as being 'famous for all kinds of wickedness'. Our imagination worked on this description but try as we might we couldn't believe ill of this sleepy seaside resort.

We were dropped off at the road end leading to the dunes and golf course and set off down to the beach where Beacon Hill looks out to sea. Some residents of the town used to be responsible for keeping watch and lighting a beacon if there was any sign of trouble such as the approach of Paul Jones, a notorious pirate who attacked Alnmouth during the 18th century.

On the tide line two breakwater posts leant together like an old couple, wrinkled and worn by time. They look out to far horizons, two 'old salts' ready to brave life together, to take whatever the sea might cast at their feet.

Lost at Sea

Quaint cottages once concealed
The fisherwives' concern.
Anxious needles crossed and clicked,
A cable's twist,
A moss stitch block,
Stocking stitched,
Identity locked,
His village clearly named
Within his sweater's
Knitted code.

We walked along the beach looking out to Coquet Island, now seeming quite close to land, and over the worn breakwaters towards Foxton. My blisters complained about a rather rocky and stony stretch causing us to make our way onto a cliff path which wound round weekend timber chalets set amongst the marram grass.

Rounding the headland we could see Boulmer in the distance, fishing cobles bobbing in its natural harbour. As we drew nearer, we discovered benches set amongst the sandy banks bordering the beach and settled down to eat our bread and cheese washed down with water. In the sea air and sunshine it tasted very good. Fishermen were working on their cobles, preparing to go to sea. The design of the fishing coble is unique to the coast between Holy Island and Flamborough, having evolved to suit surf conditions and flat sandy beaches. It has a flat bottom, a sharp, deep fore-foot, a slender body and will take a small sail. Its balanced oars have narrow blades to reduce resistance. Usually cobles are manned by two fishermen but can take up to four. While we watched, a tractor was hooked up to the coble's trolley and it was towed down to the sea.

'Harry, did you know that each village on the Northumbrian Coast has its own knitting pattern?' I think Harry thought, 'That's just the kind of useless bit of information I need right now,' because he just responded with a grunt. 'It's to identify the men. If they're lost at sea their rescuers will know which village they came from. I don't know whether women still do it today, so few people knit at all, but it's quite clever really, better than a person's name which could belong anywhere.'

A little way inland is RAF Boulmer, the air sea rescue service in this area. Their bright yellow helicopters are often seen patrolling the skies, sometimes out on an emergency, sometimes on a training exercise but their presence is always reassuring.

The next section of our walk was one well known to us and loved as a favourite stretch of coast. Here, beyond Boulmer, lies a delightful bay with a pure white beach aptly named Sugar Sands. Very often we walk here and find no trace of footprints. In winter, the tide line is alive with wading birds. Today two or three families enjoyed a quiet, private afternoon. We exchanged 'hellos' as we passed heading for a footbridge over a wooded inlet. At this point a path leads inland through tall, silver-barked beech trees. This was once the access route to the beach for residents at Howick Hall. Earl Grey, one of a great land owning Northumbrian family and previous owner of Howick Hall, became Prime Minister. In the 1830's he condemned the rotten boroughs where corrupt practices made elections a mockery. He observed the discontent in France which led to the French Revolution, afraid that a similar uprising might occur in Britain. He pledged to introduce political reforms but his bill was defeated again and again. The country was in a state of unrest. Eventually the King, William lV, was persuaded to allow Grey to create sufficient peers to enable the bill to be passed and at last his reforms became law, a constitutional model for the world.

We crossed the footbridge and stood looking upstream through the tall beech trees which are part of the Chinese Valley and lead to the Silver Wood planted to celebrate the previous Lord Howick's Silver Wedding. The current Lord Howick is a keen gardener and has been on numerous expeditions to China collecting seeds from the wild. He is currently taking part in a botanical study monitoring the progress of specimens taken from China to be nurtured in three very different environments, Kew, Howick and California. A walk around his fifteen acres of garden is a delightful experience, but not for us today. We crossed over the footbridge and, looking back, took a photograph of this delightful bay. It must be another to add to a collection we already have, but it is so photogenic it is difficult to resist taking just one more.

Our path led through tall gorse with linnets singing in the sunshine. Lower branches on the gorse were stripped bare by the ravages of salt laden air and prevailing sea breezes.

Out at sea, a rock was a basking place for seven cormorants who stood with outstretched wings drying their feathers in the sunshine. Thyme, thrift and harebells flourished in the sandy soil and grasses whispered in the wind.

Red sandstone rocks jut out into the sea near a house perched on the cliffs beside the path. This house is known as 'The Bathing House' because inmates of Howick Hall used it for changing their clothes before taking a bathe in the rocky bay at its feet. I believe it was also used by Queen Victoria when she stayed as a guest of the Duke of Northumberland at Alnwick Castle. It has recently been restored and is now a holiday cottage available for rent. I sat on a rock for a few minutes musing about what it must be like to live there right above the sea. Waves turned peacefully onto the shore of this perfectly formed ellipse and larks sang in the grasses behind me.

Beyond the Bathing House, the path winds along the cliffs between brambles and hawthorn. In the rocks below is Rumbling Kern, a blowhole through which the sea is forced with tremendous power producing awesome thundering roars. The cliff top path continues to Howick Scar, part of the Whin Sill which protrudes out to sea providing inviting ledges for nesting kittiwakes, and then across short turf towards Craster.

The Bathing House

A single house perched above
A tiny bay, scooped out
As though some hand
Had cupped and cast away the sand.
By day, a pleasant
Place to sit and muse.
At night, four walls,
Closed against the world,
Feel the tide
Batter the cliffs,
Crashing
Crushing from the mind
All thoughts
Save, 'Will the house stand?'

A Safe Return

Harbour walls embrace
Each coble's safe return.
They gather every vessel
From the sea
With great relief,
As though they were
A lover, sweetheart, wife.
Thankful to know
Their dear one's home
And now lies rocked to sleep,
Safe cradled in their arms.

We ate an ice cream on a seat overlooking the quaint harbour of Craster, enjoying the late afternoon sunshine. The harbour was built by the Craster family in memory of a brother who died on active service in Tibet. A strange memorial. Craster is famous for its delicious kippers and a pungent smell from Robson's smoke house hung on the air. People dawdled quietly about. It was all very pleasant. But we would have to press on since our room for the night was in Dunstan, a mile and a half inland. We set off past lovely cottage gardens bright with poppies and roses. We called at a nearby café and had some sandwiches made up ready for the next day then continued a laboured trudge up the road with Dunstan perched above us. Perhaps tonight our en-suite bathroom would hold the luxury of a bath where I could really give my feet a good soak. I could only hope.

'Stonecroft' was a large, modern bungalow. We were shown to a pleasant room, tastefully decorated with neat drapes and a sparkling en-suite bathroom alas with only a shower. Almost next door, was 'The Cottage Inn', a very popular hostelry serving excellent bar meals. I had Mexican Chicken followed by hot Morello Cherries and ice cream while Harry enjoyed Boeuf Bourguignonne and Drambuie trifle.

Craster looking north

Day 4
Craster
to Bamburgh

Next morning dawned bright and sunny. Our first landmark for today was Dunstanburgh Castle. I can remember my first tantalising glimpse of Dunstanburgh from a car travelling along the coast road, wondering how to get closer to this romantic ruin. Now I know that a grassy track from Craster or along the beach from Embleton are the only access points. In Craster we joined Sunday walkers all making their way towards the stunning remains of Dunstanburgh. What makes this castle so romantic…so imposing ? It stands on an outcrop of the Whin Sill. Its towers and ramparts rear up against a backdrop of blue sky and waves pound cliffs and rocks at its feet. Our delightful grassy track led us on beside the sea with the castle always in view. Two huge drum towers, which were part of the gatehouse, dominate the walk. Just before the track climbs up to the towers it dips down to cross what used to be a harbour, a deep, narrow inlet. A ditch dug in 1314 extended this natural harbour into a moat which effectively made an island of the promontory on which the castle stands. The castle was built by the Earl of Lancaster in 1313. He was an ambitious man

constantly challenging the King - Edward ll. Perhaps Lancaster looked on Dunstanburgh as a place of refuge, a bolt hole in times of trouble. However he was never to shelter within its walls. He was executed for treason, and the King gave the Castle to Roger Horsley, his steward in the North. Another famous and romantic owner of the castle was John of Gaunt who ordered many changes to its structure and in 1384 led an invasion of Scotland from its walls. After John of Gaunt's death it passed through many hands until, in 1550, it was described as being 'in a wonderful great decaye' Turner painted this picturesque ruin three times. His sketches and watercolours can be seen in Tate Britain.

Much of the stone in Northumberland is sandstone dating from a time when the coastal area was under the sea. Lava from volcanoes in the Cheviot Hills forced its way through cracks in the sandstone, cooling and hardening into black volcanic rock known as the Whin Sill which is seen in many ridges throughout the county. Dunstanburgh stands on one of these ridges and, on the north side, cliffs plunge a hundred feet down to the sea where rocks have been eroded into a funnel and rumbling waves surge up, spouting spray even as high as the castle itself - this is Rumbling Churn. On the beach lies a large saddle shaped rock of interest to geologists.

Dunstanburgh

Dunstanburgh's romantic ruin
Sits atop a waved lashed shore
Where winter gales resound
Around
Its roofless halls.
In summer, skylarks spill
Their precious silver song above its walls.
These riches freely given
Make monarchs of us all.

Kathleen Gilbert

57

Locals believe that it was used as a landing stage by smugglers. Search on the beach around here and you may find some Dunstanburgh diamonds - pieces of prettily coloured quartz.

A friend who used to live in Craster told me that the time to visit the castle is at night when there is a full moon. Then you may be able to see the ghost…. the white lady who sleeps under an evil spell, waiting for her knight to release her when he will receive the Dunstanburgh diamonds as his reward. Dunstanburgh a place wound round with mystery and romance.

I can't look at the cliffs below Dunstanburgh Castle without remembering that it was here in my youth that I began to realise that wearing your collar the wrong way round does not automatically make you sensible, responsible or innately different from those who conform to normal codes of dress.
We were members of the local Methodist Youth Fellowship and had joined with our opposite numbers from Seaton Delaval for a day at this historically rich part of the coast. We were accompanied by two gentlemen of the cloth, the Reverends Bob Delap and Tom Duerden. Kath and I had emerged from our exploration of the castle when we became aware that some of the group were on the beach below the cliffs on which the castle is built, so we worked our way down the slopes to the north to join them. Now, where

physical danger is involved, I am no risk taker so I was quite shocked and somewhat apprehensive to find two people, still clad in open raincoats, halfway up the cliff face apparently demonstrating the difficulty of attacking the castle from the seaward side. Imagine my surprise to learn that the rock climbers were our spiritual leaders. I never did discover whether it was a demonstration of faith or a plan to deliver their own version of "the sermon on the mount" but I'm sure it did their 'street cred'. no harm. H

We skirted the confines of the castle and re-joined the shore at Embleton Bay, a wide, richly golden, sandy beach. Once more we 'plodged' through streamlets joining the sea, walking sometimes through the dunes, sometimes on the shore.

A track leads from the dunes to Embleton village. Here in Embleton Church are windows and memorial tablets dedicated to the Greys of Falloden, each bearing their emblem, a scaling ladder. The most famous member of the family was Edward, Viscount Grey, the great - great - nephew of Charles Grey, the prime minister who introduced the reform bill. Edward Grey became foreign minister and in 1914 delivered a widely acclaimed speech persuading the Commons that Britain should honour its commitments to Belgium and go to war with Germany. This was against all his principles. He was a peace loving man and had striven to preserve peace in Europe. 'I hate war..I hate war,' he declared, feeling that he had failed in all his efforts. Throughout the war, he kept on good terms with neutral countries such as Sweden and the United States. They respected his honesty and fairness. He hoped that after the war there might be a chance to build a league of nations to preserve the peace of mankind. As foreign minister he worked tirelessly but at great cost to himself, for his eyesight deteriorated quite rapidly. He was advised to take holidays and rest his eyes but he continued to pour over paper work. Finally in December 1916, having become almost blind, he had to resign. He returned to his beloved home at Fallodon but was unable to see his favourite places or the birds he loved so dearly. He could hear the beautiful bubbling notes of the curlew but could not see the purple heather or the swelling Cheviot Hills, blue on the horizon. With the help of a friend, Mr Henry Herbert, he wrote a book called, 'The Charm of Birds' which describes the variety of songs and calls of birds of Fallodon throughout the seasons. 'Troubles come not single spies' was certainly true for Edward Grey. In 1917 Falloden was burned down, eventually to be rebuilt on a smaller scale. In 1928, his second wife, Lady Pamela, died quite suddenly and in the same year his brother Charles was killed by a buffalo in Africa. His personal problems and his sense of failure on the world stage however, never defeated him. He faced life with courage and humour, determined to make the best of what was left to him. Fallodon Hall, lies two miles inland from Embleton but is not open to the public.

At the far end of the Bay we encountered Sunday trippers again, this time at Low Newton. Scattered among the dunes here are weekend chalets. Beyond them is a lake, part of a reserve owned by the National Trust. Outside the ladies toilet, a man stood beside a telescope on a tripod. I felt like telling him he was looking for the wrong type of bird but thought better of it.

Our path went on, this time over rolling cliffs. Here I met the secretary of the art club I belong to. We greeted each other as though we were in a foreign country - well here was proof that we were actually doing the walk. Our bright and sunny morning had turned suddenly chilly. It was long past twelve o'clock but since Newton we hadn't found a sheltered place for our lunch break. We pressed on, one and a quarter miles to Beadnell - we'd stop there. Eventually we arrived at Beadnell harbour, the only harbour on the east coast to face west. A group of eighteenth century lime kilns stand beyond the harbour walls, their sturdy stonework penetrated by arched passageways used by fishermen to store lobster pots. We could find no protection from the wind. Our only prospect of shelter seemed to be below the sea wall, so we made our way, gingerly in my case, over bruising pebbles and sat in the stored heat of the concrete wall where we gratefully ate our sandwiches.

Later, a small shop yielded what was more precious to me than gold - elastoplasts. Since Lynemouth there had been no pharmacies and nowhere to get new medical supplies for those blisters. Then we were off once more into a stiff breeze towards our next staging post.

Seahouses is a brash, tawdry place of ice creams, fish and chips, children's money-in-the-box rides on neighing horses, lettered rock, and boat trips to the Farne Islands, all bright and cheerful. A place of day trippers, motor bikes and caravans. There's nothing better than to sit on a seat overlooking Seahouses Harbour and eat fish and chips from the paper. You might have to share them, willingly or not, with the local flying felons.

In the days before everybody owned a car, my boyfriend of the time and I used to hitch-hike from Gosforth to this part of the Northumbrian Coast. We would only stay for the day but loved the area and came to believe that it had its own weather, it was always bright and sunny.

Eating Fish and Chips above Seahouses Harbour

I have happy memories of clambering aboard one of Billy Shiel's boats and sailing across to the Farnes. They are magical islands to those who love birds. Terns swoop and dive overhead threatening to gouge pieces of flesh from unprotected heads; puffins return to nest holes with beak loads of sprats ranged head to tail; grey seals raise their heads above water, peering curiously at tourists in bobbing boats and everywhere is the clamour and smell of seabirds and an air of excitement and activity. It's wonderful to lie on the warm, sea washed turf, looking up at a blue sky and it's easy to feel at one with St. Cuthbert who spent years here alone, in harmony with his creator and the natural world.

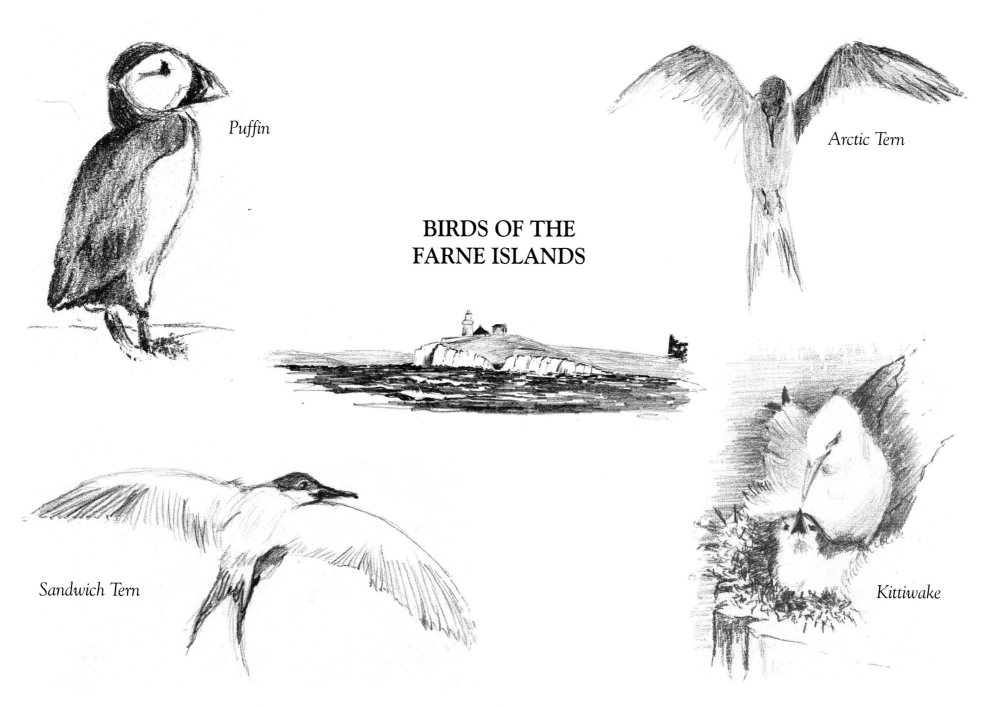

Puffin

Arctic Tern

**BIRDS OF THE
FARNE ISLANDS**

Sandwich Tern

Kittiwake

A friend, Mark, told us about going out of Seahouses Harbour to fish.

'We went out night fishing in the current between Holy Island and Bamburgh. You can catch lovely cod out there but only for an hour. I put an envelope through the harbour master's letter box in Seahouses with our harbour fees in it saying we would be fishing off Bamburgh. It was four o'clock in the morning when - Bang! We seemed to hit something but couldn't see anything in the water. All the forward gears had gone. We thought we'd better put it in reverse and go back to Seahouses, then - Bang! Reverse gear went as well. There we were bobbing up and down, Bamburgh Castle appearing and disappearing. Then I looked round, 'What are you doing?' I said to me mate.

'Sending off a rocket ..what else?'

And off it went. 'Whoosh!' 1200 feet up. 1200 feet! You'd think somebody would have seen that! We waited…. and waited. I expected to see the helicopter come over the horizon but there was nothing. And we just bobbed up and down, Bamburgh Castle appearing and disappearing. Then we sent up four rockets…four rockets! Still nothing. By this time folks were out on the beach walking their dogs. They must have seen us. Then suddenly, 'Boom!' The maroon from Seahouses went off. They came out in the dingy. We threw them our rope. We would have been claimed as salvage if we had taken theirs. I tried to keep the name of the boat quiet. I didn't want the embarrassment of it being reported in the papers. We got to Seahouses harbour and there, on the slipway was 'the big boat', the lifeboat, with its crew all kitted up. All ready to look for us. We'd done this! I could have crawled away and hid. And the press did get hold of the name of the boat.

'Hev ye seen this in the paper? Boat been rescued off Bamburgh,' a mate said to me in the pub the next night, and he just sucked on his pipe with a knowing look.'

We left busy Seahouses and walked on to stay with its more sedate neighbour - Bamburgh. The wind whipped up white horses and changed the sea to jade green. Inner Farne Lighthouse was brilliant white against navy blue clouds and the wind carded sand in flowing braids. Shining bright on the horizon was the red and white striped Longstone Lighthouse where Grace Darling once lived. On our landward side, high dunes of white sand towered against dark clouds and there, between them, were the proud walls of Bamburgh Castle. It's not surprising that this stretch of coastline has been used as a location for many films, among them El Cid. It is so picturesque.

The Castle was described by Walter Scott as 'King Ida's Castle huge and square'. It is a spectacular and romantic image sitting atop the outcrop of Whin Sill, unassailable on all sides, looking out over a sandy shore and the dangerous waters around the Farne Islands on one side and dominating the village of Bamburgh on the other. It was one of a chain of castles built against invasion from the sea. The others were at Berwick and Lindisfarne in the north and Warkworth, Dunstanburgh and Tynemouth to the south. Bamburgh was the centre of a kingdom stretching as far south as the Humber and was a Christian focus in a pagan land. In the 7th century Bamburgh was set alight by Penda, King of Mercia but it was believed that the prayers of St. Aidan in his cell on the Farne Islands caused a change of wind and the settlement was spared further damage. During Norman times the castle was rebuilt in stone which was carried on horseback from North Sunderland. During the Wars of the Roses the castle was besieged and badly damaged by cannon fire but the massive keep, built of walls nine to ten feet thick, has survived to this day. Lord Armstrong of Cragside bought the castle in 1894 and instigated extensive restoration work with the aim of converting what was a partly ruined structure into a convalescent home in memory of his wife.

We rang the bell at Green Gates. We could hear a phone ringing then the door opened.
'Oh! Wow! What a colour. Gosh that's bright. I like bright colours. I like green. They're great. I like them. Tenson' Claire, our next hostess, was referring to our matching Tenson Waterproofs in an almost luminous pea green.
'The walkers,' she continued. 'Where are you walking to? To some people a walk is just round the village. To others it's 260 miles. One couple started down in Yorkshire and were going into Scotland, then down to the Lake District.
Still, Tynemouth to Berwick…that's a walk. Welcome to the madhouse. I'll show you to your room.'
We went in and were immediately confronted by a view of Bamburgh Castle up front and filling the entire window. I found myself echoing Claire's words, 'Wow! What a view.'

Wow! What a View - Bamburgh Castle

'That's the basin,' Claire went on, giving us a tour of the facilities. Then as we began discarding the pea greens, there was more admiration. 'They were in a sale at Fishers in Keswick. We'll sell them to you for…..er…. Let's say £150.' There was more banter.

'I'll show you the rest of the facilities.' We followed her down a few steps to a landing. 'That's…. Well that's IT,' she said pointing to the W.C. with door standing open and stating the obvious. 'And next door's the shower. I think you'll find between one and two will be hot enough,' pointing to the thermostat. 'Downstairs is the resident's lounge.'

We went into a large, high room with windows on two sides. Through one we could see the Bamburgh Sunday cricket match on the green, while in the other, the red sandstone walls of the castle filled the frame. We sat on a soft velveteen sofa facing the cricket match. Our hostess was a slim, bubbly, brunette wearing shorts, sweatshirt and trainers.

'Right. Breakfast is Bamburgh home cured bacon, sausages made in Bamburgh, tomatoes, mushrooms and egg. Now, would you like a cup of tea and a slab of toast and marmalade? The marmalade's home made in Bamburgh. Well, made by my friend.'

We could hear the phone ringing in the distance. We attempted to say 'Yes' but hardly got it out before Claire was off again.

'The tea will be 2 minutes.'

It was good to sink into the welcome embrace of the sofa and remove the trainers along with a pound or two of sand emptied into the waste bin.

Our hostess returned with a teapot and a plate of great wedges of toast spread an inch thick with Bamburgh home made marmalade. It was good.

On the outskirts of the village is the Church of St. Aidan which dates from the 13th century. It stands on the site of a previous wooden church built by the missionary, Aidan. A beam in the church is believed to have survived from that time. Legends say that Aidan leant against that beam when he died. Fires destroyed future buildings but the power of the saint protected the beam which never burnt.

The church has many interesting architectural features but is perhaps best known for a monument in the churchyard commemorating Grace Darling who, on a stormy night in 1838, rowed out with her father from Longstone Lighthouse on the Farne Islands, to rescue the survivors of the 'Forfarshire', which had run aground on Harcar Rocks, a mile away. The vessel was sailing from Hull to Dundee but had a damaged boiler. Mr. Darling offered, by morse code, to go to their aid but the Captain refused. Next morning Grace could hear cries for help and she and her father saw five passengers and four members of the crew clinging onto the fore part of the ship. They launched the lifeboat and together rowed against tumultuous seas to rescue them. It's sad that Grace managed to perform this heroic deed but died of tuberculosis only four years later at the age of twenty six.

A small museum to her memory is situated opposite the church. It contains only memorabilia pertinent to Grace Darling. Standing proudly in a glass case is the actual lifeboat used by Grace and her father. The coble looks large and heavy. I remember wondering at the amount of effort it must have taken for one man and a young woman to row, through rough seas, to rescue the survivors. A framed report from the Newcastle Evening Chronicle hangs on the wall. It was printed ten days after the rescue, the length of time it took for this 'melancholy intelligence' to arrive. Over five hundred ships have been wrecked in waters surrounding the Farne or Fern Islands, some of them sunk by torpedoes during the second world war. Longstone Light still shines to warn mariners of these dangerous waters.

That night we ate at the Queen Victoria at the top of Front Street. The only bar table vacant, faced the pool table and we were entertained by a father and son having a game together. 'There Dad. Take that one.' said the son. 'That's good Daddy.' He was a boy of about nine or ten and had his own cue. He obviously liked the attention of an audience but it was nice to see a father and son with a positive relationship sharing something other than watching television. We suspect that Dad wasn't exactly playing to win.

Grace Darling's Memorial

Bamburgh Village and Castle

Day 5
Bamburgh to
Holy Island

'**M**orning gang and how are you guys?' We muttered something about fine.

'Good man. Now, sausage, egg, bacon, mushrooms, tomatoes. Alright?'

'Yes…yes fine. I'm afraid we've left some sand on the bedroom carpet.'

'Sand and grass when they cut the…No…No… No. I'd be worried if there wasn't. Think nothing of it. Now are you tea people or coffee?'

'Oh, tea thank you'

We ate breakfast at a long, sun bleached table in the window of the residents lounge facing the green, watched by Claire's daughter Zoe, who was ready for school and waiting for her school bus which would take her to the nearest middle school in Ellington, 7 miles away. Other guests, a couple from York and another from Oxford, joined us. We talked about the area. The people from York hadn't been to Northumberland before but the couple from Oxford were frequent visitors and had stayed with Claire previously. Our hostess re-entered carrying a huge plate of thick toast.

'Here you are boys and girls. Grab a slab.'

And to our murmured thanks she replied, 'You're more than welcome.'

The phone rang. The lady from Oxford said, 'Oh there's the parrot again. It does a wonderful imitation of a ringing phone.' Realisation dawned in our minds and we wondered how Claire managed to distinguish between the real phone and the parrot.

After breakfast we went to pay.

'The butcher has just made some buns,' said Claire with the phone in her hand. 'How many would you like him to keep for you?' And Claire relayed to someone on the other end of the phone that we would like two baps.

'I was admiring the paintings on your walls.'

There were a number of watercolours all signed Paul Manson. Manson being Claire's surname I was curious to discover the connection.

'Yes. By my ex. He seems to have forgotten about them. That's alright by me. He was a glass blower.'

I remarked that you could detect that influence in the paintings - the fused curling patterns.

'Now he's a fireman.'

We left to the sound of the phone ringing - or was it just a good imitation. We'll never know.

Carter's, the butcher's shop, was at the top of Front Street. We presented ourselves and said that Claire had sent us. Two very healthy sized ham sandwiches were made up for each of us, then we set off along The Wyndings, a narrow street

Bamburgh Castle

Picture
A proud, majestic, castle
Set between sea and sky,
Square walls ablush as with a sunset's glow
Are girdled by a ring of dunes,
At its feet lie glistening sands
And waves which toss their milky manes
Against an azure sky.
A joyous fanfare rips the air,
As geese fly north to Budle Bay,
Proclaiming loudly,
'This is Oswald's land,'
This blessed land
This Kingdom by the Sea.

leading to dunes which create a sandy foreground to a classic view of Bamburgh Castle. Scattered amongst the dunes are a few remaining bathing huts. A lighthouse stands on Budle Point. On the rocks below is a painting of a white stag which is retouched whenever the lighthouse is painted. No-one seems to know the origins of this work of art. We headed through the golf course towards Budle Bay. It was a glorious morning and views across the Bay towards Holy Island were stunning. White sand shimmered to far horizons, sunlight glistened on shallow water and the sky was a cavern of blue arcing over our heads. Holy Island looked remarkably close. We made our way through the dunes and down to the estuary flats of Budle Bay, passing patches of yellow irises and sea pinks and a group of eider ducks with twenty-eight chicks. Redshanks piped, curlews gave their plaintive call and larks rose up from the dunes climbing higher and higher amidst a shower of sound.

Walking on sticky estuary mud and slimy stones became difficult so, at Waren Mill, we climbed the bank onto the road. The mill was in a sorry state of picturesque dereliction with weeds sprouting from gutters and colonising stonework. It was built by the Admiralty in 1783 to provide farmers with an outlet for their wheat. When we re-visited recently, we discovered that the building is being renovated and made into apartments. An ideal 'pad' for an ornithologist.

Here at the head of Budle Bay was a road junction with a signpost. We stopped in our tracks, unbelieving. It said Berwick 15 miles, Holy Island 14. It was now 11 a.m. Walking on the tussock grass and pebbles had been hard going on my blistered feet. There was no way I could now walk 14 miles. Perhaps it was shorter round the coast which is what we had intended doing. We interrupted a farmer who was working on his tractor in a nearby field.
'Is there a way round Budle Bay on the coast?' we asked.
He sucked on his pipe.
'Wouldn't do that,' he said. 'Can be dangerous. Party was stranded a little while ago. Had a struggle to get back. There's some dangerous mud flats. Coast Guards can't use helicopters there. Suction of mud and a tight rope would pull a body in two. It's a hell of a long way round. Go by road.'
Returning his pipe to his mouth he made off back to his tractor.

Disillusioned, we stood in a quandary. What to do now? We consulted a bus timetable I had collected at Dunstan. There was a bus stop at Waren Mill and a bus, which would take us to the Holy Island road end, but it was not due for another two hours, which would make us late crossing the causeway. We could ring the 'Crown and Anchor' on Holy Island, cancel our booking and stay on the mainland somewhere but we had paid a deposit and anyway I liked the idea of spending a night on the island.

A taxi might be an idea. We went to a nearby phone box but there were no adverts for taxis and no phone book. How about knocking on a nearby cottage door to ask to borrow their phone book. We looked but there was nobody about. They were probably holiday cottages.
'We could hitch.' I said. 'This is quite a good place. Cars come round the bend, over the rise, see us straight ahead and there's somewhere to pull off the road.' The words were hardly out of my mouth when a car appeared on the rise.
'Yes? Yes.' I put out my thumb and the silver car slowed to a stop.
'Where are you going?'
'Holy Island road end?'
'Yes, I can do that. Hop in.' Clothes and other belongings were re-arranged and we got in. They were a Yorkshire couple staying at Craster and exploring the area for the first time. We told them what we were doing.
'And what's waiting for you at the end of your journey?'
'A big bath,' I replied without hesitation.
They dropped us near Beal and we set off to walk down the road to the causeway. We were exhilarated. We had used our wits and got out of a problem. I was delighted to find my skills as a hitchhiker had not deserted me. It was fine, breezy and sunny. Bamburgh Castle was a navy blue outline on the horizon. Harry sang 'Fishermen of England' and I trailed my hands through the tall purple grasses and 'old man's baccy' at the side of the road. Blisters were forgotten for a while.

There was a small gathering of cars and delivery vans parked near the causeway watching the tide recede, waiting for the time when they could 'chance' a crossing. Knowing that we would be among the last to be able to cross, we settled down in the shelter of a concrete defence block and ate our sandwiches. Carter's ham and new baked baps tasted very good. I mused on the fact that this area had been mined and used as a defence training area during the Second World War, and on the notices that warned of still unexploded mines. I wondered just how dangerous it was to walk along the mud flats. Harry did a 'recky' in preparation for next morning, following a path which hugged the shoreline. He came back to tell me that it went around the headland to a bridge, which crossed yet another inlet. We could follow that next day.

There was a roar as the engine of a motor bike was revved up and then cut off. We stood up and looked out from our concrete defence block to see a brilliantly shining Harley Davison had pulled up behind us. Its owner was dismounting and removing his black, Darth Vader type helmet. He nodded in our direction and surveyed the rest of the parking area then looked across to a line of traffic gathering where a swirling tide was gradually revealing the causeway.

'Keen to be off as usual,' he said, indicating in their direction. 'Doesn't pay to chance it. There's a horrific current comes round the top of Scotland and there's nothing to stop it till it hits the island. It's a wall of water that will take a car clean off the causeway.'

We were stunned into an awed silence. Harry recovered first and said, 'You know this part of the world then?'

'Yes, I'm a coast guard for this area. Believe me it can be pretty dangerous.' We didn't doubt him for one moment. 'There was a foreign family caught on the causeway. They couldn't read the signpost. Thought it was one of those quaint British things called a ford and kept going till the water started to come in over the top. Fortunately they made it to the box,' he indicated a dirty white structure like a hen coup on tall poles, the refuge box.

'Not the most pleasant place to be. It's used as a toilet. It can be a case of desperation if you are stuck up there for several hours with the North Sea all around you. But it does have a telephone. The helicopter lifted them off. This is my patch,' he added proprietorially as he surveyed the scene.

'Is this a full time job then?' I asked.

'No…no…I'm a teacher for my sins and part time coast guard on pager call. It's a two tier system. We have Initial Response Teams - IRTS - who are on the scene in twenty minutes and can have a helicopter to the incident in ten to twelve minutes. They can also call one of the Back Up Response Teams - BURTS - if they deem it necessary. Somebody wanted to call us the Fast Action Response Team but we decided against that. He paused to let it sink in then laughed as he saw realisation dawn on our faces. 'Well you've got to lighten the mood haven't you. I always say to them when we arrive on the scene, Some people will do anything for a ride in a helicopter.'

I tried to imagine being greeted with this epithet but try as I might I couldn't believe that, if I was in some dire predicament, my sense of humour would be up to the challenge.

'We're walking up the coast,' I volunteered, 'From Tynemouth to Berwick.'

'Well I hope you kept out of the mud round Fenham Flats. It stinks round there…birds seem to love it.'

'Are there really unexploded bombs on this stretch of coast?' I asked indicating the path on the north side of the causeway.

'Goswick Sands? Oh yes, it was a big bombing range in the second world war. Huge amount of ordinance. Occasionally we have to call the bomb squad from Rosyth. They're crazy. They came out one time for a mine that had been washed up.

They just dragged it across the beach with a tractor to where they wanted it. When they blew it up it left a hole as big as a house.'

He was feeding on our curiosity.

'We once had a report that the beach was on fire. A Jack Russel had scratched up an old phosphorus grenade which started burning. The bomb squad couldn't get there 'til next morning so we were told to guard it. When the squad did arrive they told us to get lost it was too dangerous. Every now and again something nasty turns up, but you'll be alright if you keep to the path.'

The causeway was rapidly beginning to appear from beneath the waves and a delivery van went across, casting up great bow waves as he went. Private cars thought better of it and waited a while longer.

'Before the causeway was built and everyone had their own car, a fleet of rusty old taxis transported people across with their luggage strapped to the running boards. They had to know where the sand was firm enough.'

'Are you on a call today?'

'No…no We've an occasional day's holiday so I'm meeting up with a diving team. All sorts of wrecks off the Farne Islands. You can even see parts of the Forfarshire - you know, of Grace Darling fame. Well, looks as though I can cross without getting too much salt water on the Harley.

Hope you manage it to Berwick.' And he donned his Darth Vader, mounted his trusty steed and left us blinded by glinting chrome.

We followed, less dramatically, in his tyre marks towards Holy Island. Bleached white sandbars marked each horizon and big skies billowed above. The land was low slung and marked only by buildings and higher ground at the southern end. This is sacred ground, the cradle of Christianity in Northumbria. A line of posts, punctuated by wooden refuge boxes, drew a straight path unerringly from the mainland to the village - The Pilgrim Way. It cut off a huge sweep of a bay and would have made a good short cut but much of it appeared to be still under water. I envisaged sandalled monks, their robes wet around the hem, moving in a long brown procession towards the place of St. Aidan's ministry. 'I wonder if they had blisters?' I thought to myself. 'I wonder if I could persuade Harry to walk the Pilgrim Way to Santiago de Compostella - better not put it to him just yet.' It seemed fitting that we were approaching this sacred place like pilgrims of old, humbly and on foot.

The Refuge Box - Holy Island Causeway

The causeway was strewn with seaweed and, at the lowest tide point, was still quite slippery. In order to avoid passing cars, we walked on the muddy sand as much as we could, bending now into a stiff breeze. We reached a white refuge box, a place where stranded travellers who had chanced a changing tide, could take shelter. It seems incredible but this still happens and from time to time people have to abandon their cars and wait for the tide to recede.

We were now on 'The Island' as it is known locally, and the road was bordered by white sand dunes. We continued to walk on the other side of the causeway, on the wet sand. In places it was awash with a sea of marsh pinks. Terns swooped and dived. A lapwing became agitated - were we near her chicks? The wind whipped our hair and tugged at our anoraks. It was a clean, scoured place. Slowly, the buildings of the village drew closer. 'The Crown and Anchor'…I wonder if there will be a bath…. a large bath of hot, soothing water to sink into,' I mused to myself as the muscles began to ache and the blisters nagged.

Our room had a four-poster bed, a wonderful view of Bamburgh Castle in the distance, a large bathroom but alas….no bath, only a shower. I sighed and began to peel off the layers of protective bandaging and toe guards. I would have to settle for a shower.

We had been asked to eat early by the girl who showed us to our room. 'You see the staff all want to watch 'The Match' so they'd appreciate it if they could finish early.' We obliged and went down to the dining area at 6-30p.m.

We ate fish and chips served by an Australian waitress. When we ordered wine she pulled a face.

'Don't you like wine?' we asked.

'Can't stand the stuff. Mix it with Coca-Cola.'

An Aussie who doesn't like wine!' we teased, and off she went for our chosen bottle.

For pudding she strongly recommended chocolate fudge cake which Harry sampled. I tried to find out how she came to get a job here on Holy Island and asked her if she was enjoying it. 'No. I'm missing my family. I'll stay for two or three weeks but then I might go to Ireland for a while before going home.'

They seemed strangely quiet locations for a young girl out to experience life in other countries. We wished her well and I privately hoped she might find some social life in Britain before she went home with her current impressions.

That evening Harry watched England versus Portugal - Euro 2000 - sitting on the bed, looking through the diaphanous drapes of the four-poster. I think he thought he'd gone to heaven and was surrounded by angel wings. I left him to it and went walk-about with my sketchpad. The Island was very quiet now that we were cut off by the tide and all the tourists had left. There was a stiff breeze and I had to find shelter in the lee of boats and walls. I looked out over the harbour towards the castle. When Henry Vlll ordered the dissolution of the monasteries, Lindisfarne Priory was destroyed and much of the stonework was used to build the castle which was to be part of the defences against the Scots. The castle was built in 1550 but in the early years of the 20th century it was made into a private home by Sir Edward Lutyens and then, in 1944, was given to the National Trust. It is in an imposing position perched on Beblowe Rock. In the distance I could see the blue outline of Bamburgh Castle which was once the seat of Oswald, King of Northumbria. He wanted Christian teachers for his kingdom and appealed to the Christian community on Iona to help him. They sent Aidan with a company of Irish monks and Oswald gave them Lindisfarne as a base. The monks established a community and went out preaching the gospel in neighbouring villages. St Aidan impressed people with his humility. Many were drawn to him and became his disciples, ready to carry on his good work.

I walked along the shore and sketched old, black, upturned boats used as stores and beach houses by the locals. When I had recorded enough information to be able to finish the drawing at some later date, I walked along the tide line looking for St. Cuthbert's beads, small fossil joints of the stone lily.

I've got some if you'd like some,' a voice said behind me.

'I was looking for St. Cuthbert's beads,' I said.

'Yes I thought that's what you were doing. We used to say that to tourists, 'I've got some if you'd like some,' and then we'd sell them.' The stranger laughed. 'I'm Joyce Wilson.'

'Hello,' I said. 'Kath Gilbert.'

Lindisfarne

Day ends.
Cuthbert's shower of stars
Rains down in shimmering light,
Bringing blessing to the earth.
Love, peace, joy
Quicken the soul,
Kindling within a rare delight.

Upturned Boats - Holy Island

'Are you staying on the Island then?'

'Just for tonight. We're walking up the coast from Tynemouth to Berwick.'

'That's a good thing to do. What made you come across to the island? You could have just gone straight up the coast?'

'I wanted to stay here and find out what it was like when the tourists had gone…to be cut off by the tide. Do you live here?'

'Not now, but I used to. My family's lived on the island for years. Dad was a fisherman so I was brought up here. Went to school on the island until I was fifteen. A teenager amongst seven and eight year olds. There were only nine pupils. It was an all age school. I got a shock when I went to technical college in Ashington where there were over a thousand students. Didn't think I'd settle at first. My father didn't want to send us to mainland schools. He thought we should be part of the island community.'

We were walking along the beach. A rising path led to the Heugh, the high ground overlooking the harbour. 'When we were children we used to picnic here amongst the primroses - it was covered with them in Spring. This whole island was our playground, a wonderful place to roam. A world of discovery. We'd plodge in the lough, go fishing for newts and frogs and make camps in the sand dunes. There's a cave where a rag and bone man used to store some of his goods but he and his cart were swept away by the tide. We believed the cave was haunted. We used to dare each other. 'Bet you wouldn't go into that cave on your own.' We'd run into the house and sit down shaking like a leaf.

'Oh yev seen Jack then hev ye?' Dad would say.

But nowadays it's all restrictions because it's owned by the National Trust. Has to be I suppose 'cos we're invaded again. First by the Vikings, now by the tourists. Locals go inside and shut their doors until the tide comes in and the tourists are gone. They retreat into themselves but you can't blame them when people come up to your window and peer in to see if there's anybody actually living in there.'

We were now sitting on a seat overlooking the Priory and beyond it towards the causeway.

'I saw a pilgrimage once. Three miles of people coming across the Pilgrim's Way, getting closer and closer. They were carrying beads and gold crosses. When they went into the Priory, we climbed up the walls to watch them. You can learn a lot by watching. We were intrigued. Full of it we were when we went home. 'Go to bed,' said father.'

'Life must have been quite hard here when you were little.'

'Yes..I suppose it was. There was no piped water on the island. We used water from a rain barrel for washing. I was fifteen when water was finally piped into the house and we had a bathroom. The Queen came you know. On Brittania. It anchored just outside the harbour and she came ashore in a barge. We were trying to raise money to renovate St. Mary's Church.' She indicated a church below us, next to the Priory. 'After that we had taps in the street. Yes, we've had all sorts of famous visitors. Kevin Whately…Flora Robson…Donald Pleasance stayed here. Roman Polanski was making a film - 'Cul-de-Sac' - Donald Pleasance rented a cottage and I did some baby sitting for his children. One night after they had been filming, he came back still wearing a white gown and lipstick. I got the fright of my life. Are you a fugitive from the football as well?'

'Yes, my husband's watching it on the T.V. in our room at the Crown and Anchor. Not my scene. I wanted some peace and quiet and to do some sketches.'

'Are you an artist then?'

'Well I enjoy painting and drawing and other people seem to enjoy looking at the results.' I showed her my sketch book.

'Very good. A nice hobby. I wish I could draw. Well I will go back and see if there's anybody ready to talk to me.'

'I've enjoyed your company.' I said and we shook hands and she headed off back down the Heugh. I watched her go off into the distance and then strolled slowly along the sandy path, looking out across the channel towards Ross Links. From here I could see the Cheviot Hills, blue in the distance. It was there in the fields that Cuthbert was tending his sheep on the night that Aidan died. He looked up into the sky and saw a multitude of falling stars. When he heard of Aidan's death he believed the stars were angels come to take Aidan to heaven. Cuthbert put his sheep in the fold and left to begin his life as a Christian. St. Cuthbert eventually became bishop of Lindisfarne, converting large numbers of heathens to Christianity. He persuaded monks to wear simple clothes of un-dyed wool and established a prayerful routine which became their way of life.

I looked out to sea beyond Bamburgh Castle and picked out islands close to the horizon - The Farne Islands. This was where Cuthbert lived in retreat for many years. He built an oratory and a cell on Inner Farne and studied birds, animals and sea creatures. Eider Ducks, commonly found along the Northumbrian shores, are fondly referred to as 'Cuddy's Ducks', in his honour. Perhaps we could call him an early conservationist. After Cuthbert's death he was buried under the altar at Lindisfarne. Eleven years later, fearing it might be taken by Viking raiders, the monks exhumed Cuthbert's body and found that it had not decayed. They adorned it with new robes and laid it in a wooden coffin which was taken to Durham Cathedral where it is still enshrined today. The monks had great influence, bringing refinement and grace to people to whom territorial tribal feuding had been a way of life. The Celtic monks had a love of curves and colours. Shortly after St. Cuthbert's death, Eadfrith, Bishop of Lindisfarne laboured to produce the magnificent Lindisfarne

Gospels, written on calf's skin with Celtic decoration and illuminated letters coloured with dyes of vegetable and mineral matter from all over the world. Eadfrith committed himself to this task as a way of honouring God and St. Cuthbert. The Gospels now reside in the British Library in London but there is an ongoing campaign to have them returned to the North East. As a gesture, a laser generated copy has been given to the Heritage Centre on Lindisfarne where it is on public display. Another copy is housed in Durham Cathedral.

I wandered down to the village and into the remains of Lindisfarne Priory. In 793 Vikings raided the Northumbrian Coast and sacked the priory. They came swiftly in the depths of winter in a surprise attack. Before any help came from the shore, they had devoured cattle, killed many of the inhabitants and sailed away with gold, jewels and monks who were likely to fetch a good price on the European slave market. Surviving monks took their sacred relics and for seven years wandered the countryside, eventually returning to Holy Island. Ten years later the priory was rebuilt by the monks of Durham. Today, pillars of rich red sandstone soar upwards from smooth green lawns. Massive columns mark the position of the north aisle. A beautiful arc, described as the Rainbow Arch, frames a semicircle of sky. I felt the island's silken peace surround me like a cocoon and I marvelled that so many holy places were here in this small but beautiful area of our county.

Back in our room, I sat on the window seat in the evening sunlight, looking out to Bamburgh Castle and set about completing the quick sketches I had done during my walk around the village.

Rainbow Arch - Lindisfarne Priory

Day 6
Holy Island to
Berwick on Tweed

We collected our sandwich order from The Island Store. 'There you are. Freshly made by my mother this morning. Oh, don't forget your postcards.'

As we came out of the shop a voice said, 'Hello Kathy, what are you doing here?' It was Peter Garven from my art group - he always calls me Kathy. We told him what we were doing.

'We're staying in our cottage - up for the summer.' He indicated an attractive, flower covered building to the left of the shop. His wife, Eleanor, heard voices and came through the garden gate to see who Peter was talking to.

'Yes, this is our cottage. I was born here…well, next door. Spent my youth on the island.'

'Did you go to school here?'

'Oh no - Had to go to Berwick to a Catholic Boarding School.' Her husky voice indicated a mischievous secret was about to be revealed. 'Helen and I put out the sacred light you know.' She paused. 'Yes, there was one of those lights, like tea lights, in a red glass holder and we leaned over the banister and spat on it and spat on it from above until it went out. They couldn't excommunicate us,' even in the re-telling she was hugging the secret to herself, full of guilty excitement, ' we weren't Catholics,' and she giggled like the schoolgirl of her lost youth.

'Not all island children went to boarding school though, did they?'

'No, some went to the all age school on the island, others went to mainland day schools but their days had to fit in with the tides and sometimes they stayed on the mainland for a night. They were taken across by horse and cart. My Grandfather used to be the postmaster for the island. He met some Americans once who were admiring the Priory. 'Aye come back next year an it'll be finished.' he told them.

She chortled in glee as she retold the story obviously rehearsed many times.

'There's allsorts goes on here you know. Our dog got pregnant - an unwanted pregnancy we'd call it these days - so my friend Helen's mother got hold of it and poured water between its legs over a big water tank in the yard. Do you know that dog had one pup and it had five legs….five legs…one was growing from its neck.' She nodded to emphasise the drama, her laughter silenced for a moment.

'It might not have looked much but it won a lot of races,' Harry pitched in with his usual corny humour.

'Where have you been staying?' Peter asked.

'The Crown and Anchor,' we replied, indicating over our shoulders to the white wall at our backs.

'Well why didn't you give us a knock? You could have stayed with us.'

'Yes You're welcome any time…any time,' said Eleanor

'Well thank you …thank you very much but we didn't know you were here….well, we'd better get going. Last leg to Berwick you know.'

There was a gale force wind blowing as we left the island. We had to bend right into it. I met a woman exercising her poodle a few yards from her car.

'Oh you're brave to be walking the causeway in this.'

'We're actually walking to Berwick.'

'Berwick. Rather you than me,' she said and I had to move on. We paused near the refuge box. The wind made visibility good.

'Look, that's it. Berwick. The Tweed.'

I could see emerald green pastures sloping down to a blue sea and just discernible was the high arched railway viaduct carrying the North East railway line across the Tweed and on into Scotland. This was our destination for tonight and the end of our walk.

The force of the wind was not quite so strong once we were on the mainland. We traced a sketchy path round the inlet and over a bridge, then on to an isolated dwelling called Beachcomber House. No one passed us. There was no one on the beach. We seemed to be the only two souls alive on that blustery morning until we reached Goswick Golf Course.

Here we were suddenly back in civilisation and our track came to an end. We had to go down to the beach. Sand was whipped from house - high dunes into our faces, scouring them as if with sandpaper. As soon as we could, we took a path into a Nature Reserve behind the dunes heading for Spittal on the outskirts of Berwick. My pace grew slower and slower. My blisters were sore. New ones were developing and my muscles ached with the effort of trying to prevent pain. How I longed for a deep, comforting bath.

Our path squeezed itself between the sea on our right and the London to Edinburgh railway line on our left. There were stunning glimpses of red sandstone cliffs and the glinting waters at the mouth of the Tweed, then below us, we saw a smart new promenade where residents of Spittal were enjoying a bracing walk. I sat on a wall in the main street resting feet and limbs.

'Hey! Listen to this,' Harry said, trying to cheer me up.

'Approaching the end of our epic journey, we have set a blistering pace and are now two feet short. Kath has been frequently plastered. No lame excuses though, as we approach the final tern. We spent last night on Holy Island in a four poster bed next to St. Aidan but Kath's pyjamas were with Claire in Bamburgh. Should coast into Berwick tomorrow where, we hope, a large bath awaits us so should make a clean getaway.'

I groaned, not sure whether this was in response to Harry's

latest epic or for my aching limbs.

'When did you compose that?'

'Oh last night during the interval in the football match.'

'Well I'm glad you put your time to good use.'

We laughed and then I rose wearily and we carried on.

Gradually the stirring sight of gracefully arching bridges across the Tweed drew closer. The railway viaduct, the Royal Border Bridge, was designed by Robert Stevenson between 1847 and 1850 and was officially opened by Queen Victoria. It has 28 arches and strides across the valley 126 feet above the river. Bridges have been of strategic importance to this border town. In times of peace they have been a link between England and Scotland, and a target in times of war between the two countries. The Tweed marks the border between England and Scotland, Berwick being the only English town north of the river. My friend Chris, who was born in the Northumbrian market town of Wooler, recalls being taken to Berwick on Saturdays to shop. 'It's a cold place Berwick. It doesn't know who it belongs to, England or Scotland. There's nothing earlier than eighteenth century. Everything was destroyed during skirmishes with the Scots.' A thriving port and market town, Berwick was a desirable possession and changed hands 13 times during its eventful history.

Entering Berwick - We'd Made It!

On Seeing Berwick-on-Tweed

A counterpane of meadows
Billows beyond
The confines of the town.
High stepping bridges
Strut gracefully
Tip-toeing above
The strife torn Tweed.
All from this cliff-top eerie seen,
Above these waves of emerald green,
Where they unfurl
And spread themselves
In shawls of frothing foam.

We could see impressive walls encircling the town. They were built around 1560 when an invasion from Scotland was expected. Two Italian engineers, Cantio and Portinari, designed the walls which are similar to those in Verona and Lucca. They looked strong and austere. I couldn't imagine anyone even thinking about attacking them.

We turned a corner and there was the old bridge, the road and footbridge spanning the Tweed. It has 15 arches each of which is an independent battlement fort expected to remain intact if the others were destroyed. It was built between 1610 and 1624 by James Burrell, Kings James 1st's surveyor. We crossed it slowly, a moment to savour, knowing that we had succeeded. We'd walked Twixt Tyne and Tweed. Our challenge was at an end.

We turned right at the end of the bridge and a few yards on came to Sally Port and our final lodgings. Elizabeth opened the door. Not the type of lady you would imagine doing bed and breakfast. She wore pink eye shadow, blue glass beads, a short straight grey skirt with a skimpy twin set and black tights. She smoothed her straight hair, bleached ash blonde, into a bunch over her shoulder as we talked. We followed her upstairs.

'So, you've been walking then?' Elizabeth enquired obviously guessing from our clothes.
'Yes, we've walked up the coast from Tynemouth.'
'Well done. That's a long way. But I think people should get out and about more. We depend too much on cars. Life is all too fast. We should slow down. I prefer a gentler pace now.'
We had reached the landing and Elizabeth led the way into a large bedroom, containing a dark oak four-poster bed.
'I used to own a restaurant in town. We won a number of awards but I was working all hours with no time for family life so I sold it all and started B&B. It's much more flexible.' Her light voice had risen to be high pitched, symbolic of the tension she had felt. 'I'm just doing this room. You have to pass through this room to get to yours but there will be nobody in here. I'm going to let it to families. I'm ironing in here at the moment. I'm roasting a chicken and making spaghetti bolognaise. Have you booked anywhere to eat tonight? Please join me if you would like to.' We went through another door and into our room. It was furnished in country pine, with a pretty white and pink duvet.
Everywhere there were arty touches; a harlequin mobile was suspended from the ceiling, bunches of dried flowers were heaped on top of the pine bookcase, a teddy bear was perched on top of a basket hamper beside the bed. But where was the bathroom? Would it have the longed for bath?

Elizabeth showed us into the room next door. Our own private bathroom and there, joy of joys, a large bath with gold plated taps and bottle on bottle of soothing bath oils. Wonderful!

There was also a guest kitchen with home made shortbread and an honesty bar. We filled in our request from the menu for breakfast; scrambled egg and smoked salmon. We made tea, then flopped on the bed for a while, mustering up the energy to move and run that longed for bath. There was plenty of hot water and the bath oils frothed and foamed. Slowly, I sank deep into the soothing waters, blissfully savouring our achievement - walking from Tyne to Tweed, walking the length of Northumberland - we'd done it!

Bliss!

FOOT- NOTE

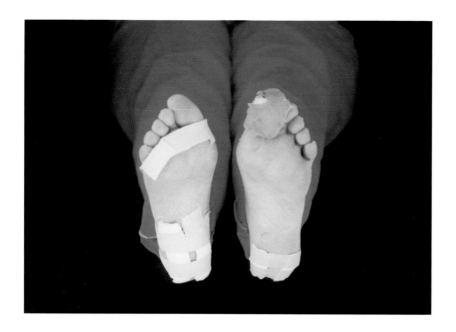

Our walk, lasting six days, covered approximately 72 miles. We made the return journey by train on the main Edinburgh - London Line, getting off at Newcastle. We then took a 'sprinter' to Cramlington Station and walked the almost 2 miles from the station to our house. When we told a friend about our exploits she said, 'Oh! Cramlington Station to your house - That's a long way!'

It's all in the mind!

REFLECTIONS

Travel changes people. Experiences on route make a difference to our perceptions. This journey was no exception. During our escapade and in the weeks and months after, when we were researching this book, we became more and more aware of the nobility and dignity of the people of our county.

We thought of the Christian monks bringing grace and civilisation to dark and troubled times and creating beauty in the form of the Lindisfarne Gospels.

We remembered the Grey family, Charles Grey struggling to introduce just and fair elections, his great-great-nephew, Viscount Edward Grey of Fallodon, in office during the first world war, paying the personal price of losing his sight in the service of his country.

Lord Collingwood, who loved the county of Northumberland but, in serving his country, never returned from the sea to spend his days here.

The Delaval and Ridley families, who were conscious of their social responsibilities and gave generously to their communities in terms of jobs, living conditions and public institutions.

In addition, there were all the people who fought against the power of the sea; Grace Darling and other less famous souls who performed brave deeds of rescue, the volunteer life brigades, the coast guards and fisherfolk who risk their lives every day around our shores, and all the multitude of ordinary folk, the miners, the shipbuilders, the fishermen and fishwives who rolled up their sleeves and with great fortitude and humour, got on with what had to be done.

Many of these people are not greatly celebrated either nationally, or locally, but they epitomise the spirit of Northumberland and together have bequeathed a rich heritage which we are proud to claim as our own.

We are thankful to live here, in Northumberland, where, in the words of Viscount Grey, 'many of the best joys in England are to be found.'

Kathleen and Harry Gilbert